Where Did I Come From?
Where Am I Going?
How Do I Get There?

Where Did I Come From?
Where Am I Going?
How Do I Get There?

Straight Answers for Young Catholics

CHARLES E. RICE AND THERESA FARNAN

Edited by Ellen Rice

SECOND EXPANDED EDITION

ST. AUGUSTINE'S PRESS
South Bend, Indiana

Manufactured in the United States of America.

1 2 3 4 5 6 14 13 12 11 10 09

Library of Congress Cataloging in Publication Data
Rice, Charles E.
Where did I come from? Where am I going? How do I get there?:
straight answers for young Catholics / Charles E. Rice
and Theresa Farnan; edited by Ellen Rice. – Rev. 2nd ed.
p. cm.
Includes bibliographical references (p.   ) and index.
ISBN-13: 978-1-58731-929-7 (paperbound: alk. paper)
ISBN-10: 1-58731-929-2 (paperbound: alk. paper)
1. Catholic youth – Religious life. 2. Catholic Church – Doctrines.
I. Farnan, Theresa. II. Rice, Ellen. III. Title.
BX2355.R455 2009
248.8'3088282 – dc22   2009002017

The Subcommittee on the Catechism, United States Conference of Catholic Bishops, has found this text, copyright 2009, to be in conformity with the *Catechism of the Catholic Church*.

Nihil Obstat:Rev. Michael Heintz, *Censor librorum*
Imprimatur: Most Rev. John M. D'Arcy,
Bishop of Fort Wayne-South Bend
11 February 2009

∞ *The paper used in this publication meets the minimum requirements of the American National Standard for Information Sciences – Permanence of Paper for Printed Materials, ANSI Z39.48-1984.*

ST. AUGUSTINE'S PRESS
www.staugustine.net

To Mary E. Rice, wife, mother, much loved –
and definitely the brains of the outfit.

To Mike Farnan, leader of the Farnan family,
with appreciation for his insightful comments and
generous encouragement that made this work possible.

To Michael Anthony, Mary Rose, Jeanne Frances,
Joseph Terence, Elizabeth Anne, Sarah Catherine,
Kathleen Mary, James Bernard, and Paul Daniel Farnan –
may they always continue to treasure the gift of our
Catholic faith.

TABLE OF CONTENTS

Acknowledgments ix

Preface x

Abbreviations xiii

1. Answer and Decide 1

2. Faith and Reason: What Are They? Can They Tell
   Me How to Live? 9

3. But Can I *Really* Know Anything? 14

4. What Can I Know about Myself? Can I *Know* Whether
   I Will Live Forever? 20

5. What Can I Know about God? Can I *Know* that God
   Even Exists? 26

6. Can I *Know* What God Is Like? 34

7. What Has God Told Me about Himself? What Does
   He Do for a Living? 41

8. Why Did God Make *Me* – and Everyone Else? 44

9. So God Made *Me* in *His* Image?! How? And What
   Difference Does It Make? 50

10. How Did It All Go Wrong? 59

11. How – And Why – Did Christ Fix the Problem? 65

12. How Is Christ with Me Today?   74

13. The Church?! Why Do I Need It?   82

14. The Natural Law? What's That All About?   89

15. What about My Conscience?   102

16. How Do I Relate to Others?   111

17. Am I a Gift to Others? What about My Freedom?   117

18. My Family – Image of the Trinity   133

19. Sex – How Did It Get So Messed Up?   141

20. The "Great Disruption": Truth *and* Consequences   153

21. So, Do I Have Rights? Where Did I Get Them?   165

22. Do I Ever Have the Right to Kill Somebody?
    What about Self-Defense?   172

23. What about Abortion?   178

24. Do We Have to Keep Grandma on a Feeding Tube
    Forever?   184

25. What about the Death Penalty?   193

26. But Can't I Kill People and Break Things in a War?   198

27. Why Is This a Great Time to Be Here?   206

Recommended Readings   214

Index   215

ACKNOWLEDGMENTS

This book project never would have got off the ground without the superb research and technical help provided by Dwight King and the other librarians of the Notre Dame Law Library, including especially Carmela Kinslow, Mary Cowsert, and Deb Fox. We are indebted to them for their generous and professional assistance.

Every institution has a person who, though underappreciated, embodies in effort, loyalty, and dedication the spirit of that institution. At Notre Dame Law School, Lois Plawecki fits that description. Lois, a faculty assistant in the Law School, now emeritus, was more than that in the preparation and organization of this book. Her management of the manuscript, from beginning to end, was indispensable and professional. And she managed to keep her sense of humor through it all. She has our utmost appreciation and respect.

PREFACE

"One cannot escape the fact that, more than in any other historical period, there is a breakdown in the process of handing on moral and religious values between generations."[1]

In saying this three years before his death, Pope John Paul II restated what is regrettably an obvious truth. Generations of Catholic children have spent their religion classes making collages or discussing politics, the environment, etc. Parents are unable to make up for the deficiency because they themselves learned nothing in the schools, as was true of their parents.

One of the blessings of the pontificate of John Paul II, however, is that he "has left behind a generation of committed young Roman Catholics who are already shaping the church in a more conservative mold."[2] This is a new breed. The operative word, however, is not "conservative," but perhaps simply "faithful." The points at issue transcend the political. They can be capsulized in the title of this book: *Where Did I Come From? Where Am I Going? How Do I Get There?* This book is written primarily, but not exclusively, for those generations drawn to the faith, or confirmed in it, by John Paul II. They will now draw further conviction from the teaching and person of Benedict XVI, who described the "purpose of dialogue" as "to discover the truth. What is the origin and destiny of mankind? What are good and evil? What awaits us at the end of our earthly existence?"[3]

Dr. Theresa Farnan and I hope that this little volume will provide some answers to those questions for young people of all ages, from students up through Generation X and beyond. Dr. Farnan is a mother of nine, a Notre Dame Ph.D. in medieval studies, an adjunct professor in philosophy at Franciscan University of Steubenville, and she has served on diocesan curriculum committees. My wife, Mary, and I hope that the reader will be impressed also, as we are, by the fact that Theresa is the seventh of our ten children. Theresa initiated the concept for this book and shaped it with unique insights and clear writing.

The theme of this book arises from John Paul II's achievement in rescuing reason and faith from the trash bin to which the Enlightenment philosophers had consigned them. "Faith and reason," said John Paul in *Fides et Ratio*, "are like two wings on which the human spirit rises to the contemplation of truth." Faith and reason are both ways of knowing. This little book aims to integrate the two so as to offer, in uncomplicated but accurate terms, an understanding of who we are, why we are here, and how we can get where we should be going.

For my part, I acknowledge my indebtedness to the late Professor Edward J. Murphy, one of the all-time great teachers at the University of Notre Dame. For nine years I was privileged to join Professor Murphy in teaching a regular religion course to seniors at Marian High School in Mishawaka, Indiana. He and I also taught, as a team, the required Jurisprudence course at Notre Dame Law School for more than a decade. I continue to teach that material at Notre Dame. This book draws upon the experience gained in those courses. On the right-to-life issues it draws also upon the insights of the late Notre Dame Law Professor Frank E. Booker, a convert to the faith. Ed Murphy and Frank Booker were superb teachers, Notre Dame men who exemplified Our Lady's University at its best. I, and generations of students, remain indebted to them.

Dr. Farnan and I offer this book in the hope and prayer that it will draw readers closer to the Truth who is a Person, Jesus Christ.

Charles E. Rice, Notre Dame, Indiana, January 1, 2009

Endnotes

1   Pope John Paul II, Address to Plenary Assembly of the Pontifical Council of Culture (March 16, 2002).

2   *New York Times* (April 14, 2005): A13.

3   Pope Benedict XVI, Address to Interreligious Meeting, Washington, D.C., April 17, 2008.

ABBREVIATIONS

In this book abbreviations are used in the footnotes for frequently cited sources. In all quotations in this book, all indicated emphases are in the original documents unless otherwise indicated.

ST   St. Thomas Aquinas, *Summa Theologica*

CA   John Paul II, *Centesimus Annus* (1991)

VS   John Paul II, *Veritatis Splendor* (1993)

LF   John Paul II, *Letter to Families* (1994)

EV   John Paul II, *Evangelium Vitae* (1995)

CCC   *Catechism of the Catholic Church* (1997)

FR   John Paul II, *Fides et Ratio* (1998)

EA   John Paul II, *Ecclesia in America* (1999)

1. ANSWER AND DECIDE

*Where have I come from and where am I going? Why is there evil? What is there after this life?[1]

"The answer to these fundamental questions," said Pope John Paul II, "decides the direction which people seek to give to their lives."[2]

We all have to answer questions and make decisions. If I am a young person moving on through high school, I will have to decide whether to go to college, enter full-time employment, serve my country in the military, or whatever else. No matter what I do, I will have to answer questions. If I go to college, the first two are standard: Where am I from? What's my major? The quick answers are: Mishawaka, Indiana, and Biology. The considered answers – I might not want to unload them on my classmates on opening day – are more basic: *Where am I from?* The answer: From God; I am his child. *What's my major?* I really mean – Where am I going and what do I want do with my life? The answer: Since I will live forever, my objective is to love God and live forever in heaven rather than in hell. As the great Doctor of the Church, Saint Thomas Aquinas (1225–1274), demonstrated, in heaven we will have the immediate presence of God, the satisfaction of all desires, the company of the blessed (of all the good people who have ever lived), and the certainty that it will never end. The alternative would be to choose not to love God, to reject him and thereby choose to live separated from Him forever in hell. (Heaven and hell could be capitalized because each is a place, just like Mishawaka).

Whatever we do with our lives, we can't really know where we're from and what we'll do with our lives unless we can answer two related questions:

Is there a God?

Is there a right and wrong?

This book will help answer these two questions. But the first thing each of us has to do is: *Use our heads.* Reason and common sense can tell us how stupid it is to claim that there is no God and no right or wrong.

1. *Use my head*

Pope John Paul II stressed the "profound and indissoluble unity between the knowledge of reason and the knowledge of faith."[3] Faith and reason are both ways of knowing. They are "like two wings on which the human spirit rises to the contemplation of truth; and God has placed in the human heart a desire to know the truth – in a word, to know himself – so that, by knowing and loving God, men and women may also come to the fullness of truth about themselves."[4]

So when we come to answer these basic questions about God and morality, we can't check our brains at the door. We have to use our heads. Thirteen days after 9/11 Pope John Paul II, in Kazakhstan, warned the leaders of that Islamic republic against a "slavish conformity" to Western culture which is in a "deepening human, spiritual and moral impoverishment" caused by "the fatal attempt to secure the good of humanity by eliminating God, the Supreme Good."[5] Pope Benedict XVI, on his visit to the United States, said "America's brand of secularism can subtly reduce religious belief to a lowest common denominator" causing a "separation of faith from life: living 'as if God did not exist.'"[6]

So, is there a God? Is there a right and wrong? Let's consider these two questions in turn.

Is there really a God?

Catholics tend to have an inferiority complex. We tend to

think the secularists are the "smart guys," that they have reasoned it all out and that our Catholic thing is only blind faith. But the fact is, it is unreasonable – even stupid – not to believe in God, the eternal Being who always existed and had no beginning. Of course there always had to be an eternal Being who had no beginning. To deny this we must say instead that there was a time where there was absolutely nothing. And we therefore must say that something can come from nothing. Actress Julie Andrews, in the motion picture, *The Sound of Music,* had it right: "Nothing comes from nothing. Nothing ever could." If there was ever a time when there was nothing, there could never be anything. If we think hard about this, it will blow our minds. And change our lives.

This book examines other ways we can know from reason

 that God exists, what he is like and what he does for a living. That God exists is discussed right away in this first chapter because it is so important for us to realize that our faith makes sense on everything, beginning with the question of God.

When we talk about God, we're not talking about some abstract theory or impersonal "life force." Rather, we're talking about a personal Creator in whose image and likeness we ourselves are made. We are talking about a God who is Love, who showed us on the cross that man "can fully discover his true self only in a sincere giving of himself."[7]

"God put us in the world to know, to love, and to serve him, and so to come to paradise."[8] The eternal happiness or "beatitude we are promised confronts us with decisive moral choices. It invites us to purify our hearts . . . and to seek the love of God above all else. It teaches us that true happiness is not found in riches or well-being, in human fame or power, or in any human achievement . . . or . . . in any creature, but in God alone, the source of every good and of all love."[9]

Only in terms of God can we make ultimate sense of everything else. As John Paul II put it, "When the sense of God is lost, the sense of man is also threatened and poisoned. . . . Without the Creator the creature would disappear. . . . [W]hen God is forgotten the creature itself grows unintelligible."[10] If there is no God, there is nothing special about man (of both sexes). And there is no basis for us to claim absolute rights against the state or anyone else. If there is no God, Adolf Hitler, the Nazi dictator, was right.

Is there really a right and wrong?

If I go to college, "Catholic" or otherwise, I will almost certainly encounter professors who are absolutely sure that they cannot be sure of anything. Or if they are not sure of that, at least they are sure they are not sure.

According to some "currents of thought which claim to be postmodern," said John Paul II, "the time of certainties is irrevocably past and the human being must learn to live in a horizon of total absence of meaning, where everything is provisional and ephemeral."[11] This culture in which we live denies the ability of reason to know an objective moral order. "Objective" means that the moral order exists in reality and does not depend on what we think about it: in other words, some actions, such as murder, theft, or adultery, are always wrong even if we think they are right.

"Relativism is . . . the only virtue," wrote cultural critic Allan Bloom, "which all primary education for more than fifty years has dedicated itself to inculcating."[12] But if we say that all things are relative, then that statement itself must be relative. Relativism, therefore, is absurd. On the contrary, there is objective truth. Reason can know truth – about God and ourselves. And reason can know that some things are contrary to nature and therefore objectively wrong no matter how we may feel about it. The extermination of Jews and others by the Nazis during World War II was wrong. Period. Let's hope that when we finish this book, we'll understand how and why all this is so.

So, when it comes to God and morality, the rule is: *use my head.* No one can con us into thinking that something can come from nothing or that whether murder is wrong depends on how we *feel* about it.

The second thing we have to do on these and related issues is: *Speak the truth.*

2. Speak the Truth

[T]he Holy Father . . . told me, "error makes its way because truth is not taught. We must teach the truth whenever we see something which is against the truth. We must teach truth, repeat it, not attacking the ones who teach errors because that would never end – they are so numerous. We have to teach the truth." He told me truth has a grace attached to it. Anytime we speak the truth, we conform to what Christ teaches and what is being taught us by the Church. Every time we stand up for the truth, there is an internal grace of God that accompanies that truth. The truth may not immediately enter in the mind and heart of those to whom we talk, but the grace of God is there and at the time they need it, God will open their heart and they will accept it. He said, error does not have grace accompanying it. It might have all the external means, but it does not have the grace of God accompanying it. This encouraged me very much.[13]

Each of us teaches the truth in actions as well as in words. When we treat people with fairness and honesty, we teach the truth about the nature and dignity of the human person. Empty rhetoric will not do it. The late American author and television preacher, Archbishop Fulton J. Sheen, often said that whenever he heard someone talking about his devotion to human rights and the poor, the first thing he wanted to know was how much he pays his housekeeper.

This doesn't mean that we adopt an aggressive, in-your-face attitude. But we can't be afraid to witness to the truth, with courtesy and kindness, even when we cannot see any practical advantage from it. We may never know, on this earth, how our witness to truth changed someone's life.

This chapter's author learned the importance of witness by the experience one college student related to him. She was pregnant, and her boyfriend talked her into having an abortion in another city. She entered the abortuary, filled out the papers, and waited her turn. She was on the table, prepped for the abortion, when she suddenly pictured the little Franciscan nun (in a habit) who was standing on the sidewalk praying the Rosary as she entered the abortuary. She thought of that nun who was praying for her, and she immediately left the place. She had the baby, placed him for adoption, and successfully resumed her life. She left the abortuary without ever saying a word to that nun. And that nun probably went home and thought she hadn't done much that day. But God responds to prayer as he knows best. And he used her witness to the truth to change the life of that student and of her unborn child. The truth has its own power. One reason is that the ultimate Truth is not an abstraction but a person: Jesus Christ.

This is a great time for followers of Christ to be here. The great Jesuit, Fr. John A. Hardon, S.J., said that John Paul II told him that the 21st century would see "the greatest renaissance of Christianity in history." One reason why such a renaissance is predictable is the recovery of reason, which began under the leadership of John Paul II and continues under Pope Benedict XVI. John Paul taught that, by using our heads to figure things out, we can actually know the truth about morality and can even know a lot about God. His successor, Benedict XVI, has taken up and carried forward that defense of the truth and our ability to know it. For five centuries, philosophers and politicians have criticized – and ultimately denied – reason as a way of knowing truth. In the process, faith also has been impoverished. "Deprived of what Revelation offers, reason has taken side tracks which expose it to the danger of losing sight of its final goal. Deprived of reason, faith has stressed feeling and experience, and so runs the . . . grave risk of withering into myth or superstition."[14]

John Paul's rescue of reason has practical significance. He reminds the Church that "if there is no ultimate truth to guide and direct political activity, then ideas and convictions can easily be manipulated for reasons of power. As history demonstrates, a democracy without values easily turns into open or thinly disguised totalitarianism."[15]

This short book is meant to encourage readers – especially young people (of any age) – to follow the lead of John Paul II and of Benedict XVI in recovering the unity of faith and reason. It can especially help young readers to use their heads and speak the truth – about God and about right and wrong. "People today," said Benedict XVI to the United States bishops, "need to be reminded of the ultimate purpose of their lives. They need to recognize that implanted within them is a deep thirst for God." "Without God," he said, "our lives are ultimately empty."[16]

So, on that first day in college, when someone asks me, "Where are you from? What's your major?" – I can tell him. All of it.

Endnotes

*NOTE: Italics are in originals, unless otherwise noted.
1 *FR*, no. 1.
2 *FR*, no. 1.
3 *FR*, no. 16.
4 *FR*, Preamble.
5 Pope John Paul II, Address to Cultural Leaders, Astana, Kazakhstan, Sept. 24, 2001.
6 Pope Benedict XVI, Response to Questions Posed by the United States Bishops, April 16, 2008.
7 Vatican II, *Gaudium et Spes (Pastoral Constitution on the Church in the Modern World)*, no. 24.
8 *CCC*, no. 1721.
9 *CCC*, no. 1723.

10 *EV*, no. 32, quoting *Gaudium et Spes*, no. 36.

11 *FR*, no. 91.

12 Allan Bloom, *The Closing of the American Mind* (New York: Simon & Schuster, 1987), 25–26.

13 Edouard Cardinal Gagnon, describing a conversation he had with Pope John Paul II. *Lay Witness* (March 1990), 6–7. See Charles E. Rice, *50 Questions on the Natural Law* (San Francisco: Ignatius, 2d ed., 1999), 391.

14 *FR*, no. 48.

15 *CA*, no. 46.

16 Pope Benedict XVI, Address to the Bishops of the United States, April 16, 2008.

2. FAITH AND REASON
WHAT ARE THEY?
CAN THEY TELL ME HOW TO LIVE?

God loves me so much that he wants me to love him and be happy with him forever in heaven. Sometimes I may wonder how I can love God when I cannot physically see him. How can I get to know him? How can I develop a close, loving relationship with God?

Some things I can know through reason . . .

Saint Thomas Aquinas reminds us that before we can love anyone, we must first know him. We can know God in two ways, each of which is a wonderful gift from him. The first gift is our reason. God created all human beings with reason, that is, with the ability to know things intellectually. Using our minds we can know certain truths about God. We can know that he exists, that he is intelligent, and that because he is intelligent, he is a person. These truths are examined in Chapters 5 and 6.

First we need to know some facts about our reason. Our reason enables us to know the truth about all kinds of things. How do we know if something we're thinking is the truth? Saint Thomas Aquinas defined truth as the "equation of thought and thing" – in other words, when our judgment about something matches the reality of the thing we are thinking about. If we look at a locomotive and say, "That is an airplane," that statement is false. But if we look at Lassie and say, "That is a dog," that statement is true.

God reveals what I can't know

Our ability to know God is limited. We cannot verify the truth of a statement about God's nature through our sense experiences. We cannot claim to understand his divine nature as we understand a car. So God, in his great love for us, chose to reveal himself to all of mankind, beginning with the Revelation of himself to Adam and Eve and including Christ's Revelation of himself in his life on earth.

Revelation contains some information that we can know using our reason, (including that God exists and the teachings of the Ten Commandments), and some information that we could never figure out on our own, like the Trinity and the Incarnation. God gave us this information because it helps us to know and love him while we are here on earth. Even though we can argue for God's existence using reason alone, we probably don't have the time or education to construct philosophical arguments. God wants us to know and love him, regardless of our educational background. In addition, we can make mistakes – God's Revelation preserves us from error and strengthens our confidence in the truths that we know about him.

God doesn't just want us to know him intellectually. He reveals himself to us so that we will come to know him personally and love him. If we think about it, those whom we love the most – our families, our friends – are also those we know the best. God wants us to know him and to love him – yet because he is divine and we are human, our reason cannot fully know him. The only way that we can know how much God loves us is through Revelation.

Different sources of Revelation

So what *is* Revelation? It is the self-communication of God. He "wants to communicate his own divine life to the men he freely created, in order to adopt them as his sons in his only-begotten Son [and] make them capable of responding to him, and of knowing him, and of loving him far beyond their own natural capacity."[1] Revelation has two distinct modes of transmission: Sacred Scripture and Tradition. The task of interpreting both has been entrusted to the Magisterium, which is the Church exercising her teaching function.[2] "Sacred Scripture is the speech of God as it is put down in writing under the breath of the Holy Spirit."[3] It includes all of the books of the Old and New Testaments. "And [Holy] *Tradition* transmits in its entirety the Word of God . . . entrusted to the Apostles by Christ the Lord and the Holy Spirit."[4] The Second Vatican Council tells us that Sacred Tradition was handed on by the apostles through their preaching, example, and the institutions they established.[5] "The first generation of Christians did not yet have a written New Testament, and the New Testament itself demonstrates the process of living Tradition."[6] Finally, God has given us the living teaching office of the Church, the Magisterium. That teaching office is exercised by the Pope and the Bishops in union with the Pope, to teach and interpret for us the Revelation contained in Sacred Scripture and Tradition. This is discussed in detail in Chapter 13.

Why should I be confident in my faith?

When we believe something because it is contained in Sacred Scripture, we are making an act of faith – we believe even if we cannot verify this belief based on sense experience or on logic alone. Nevertheless, belief based on Revelation *is* certain. We can point to many signs that strengthen our faith, including the witness of martyrs, the rapid spread of the faith, and the signs and miracles worked by Christ and his followers. These signs are important to us because they reinforce our belief, but they are not the most important reason for belief. We believe God's revelation because it is revealed by One who is Perfection and Goodness, who is Truth itself. God cannot lie or be mistaken because he *is* the Truth.

Why have so many people been willing to die for Christ? Love. The Mexican priest, Blessed Miguel Pro, faced a firing squad in 1927, with "his crucifix in one hand and his rosary in the other and with arms outstretched in the form of a cross." His last words were a cry, not of despair but of love and triumph – "!Viva Cristo Rey!" – "Long live Christ the King!"[7]

At the age of nine, Saint Maximilian Kolbe had a vision of the Blessed Mother in which she offered him two crowns, a white one for purity and a red one for martyrdom. She asked him which one he wanted. He said he wanted both.[8] In the Nazi death camp at Auschwitz, Fr. Kolbe volunteered to take the place of a fellow prisoner, a married man with a family, who had been selected for the "starvation bunker" in reprisal for the escape of a prisoner. Another prisoner, who was assigned the task of removing each morning the bodies of those who had died of starvation and thirst during the night, testified later, "Never have I seen anything like this. Whereas, in the past, howling and curses reverberated from the starvation bunkers like a scene of the damned in hell, this time the condemned prisoners did not curse and tear at each other, but sang and prayed. Soon the condemned in the other cells joined in the singing of hymns to Our Lady. What had formerly been a place of torment and bedlam became a place of divine worship. As if in choir, they answered one another from cell to cell with prayers. A holy saintly priest was with them to share their suffering, to counsel, encourage, and hear their confessions." Because the guards needed the cell for other victims, they killed Fr. Kolbe with an injection on August 14, 1941, the eve of the feast of Mary's Assumption.[9]

Christian martyrs, like Blessed Miguel Pro and Saint Maximilian Kolbe, do not die for an idea or in memory of some historical figure. They die for a living person whom they know and love. Martyrs can know through reason that God exists, but they come to know him personally and to love him through Revelation and the gift of faith which the grace of the Holy Spirit bestows on them. They have the certainty that comes from this personal loving relationship. As we deepen our relationship with Christ, we will enjoy the unshakeable conviction that comes from a deep and personal bond of love. God responds to our faith in him with an outpouring of grace that strengthens our faith. As we see his love guiding us throughout our lives, our own love of him deepens and begins to permeate every aspect of our lives. God gives us the gifts of faith and reason so that we can know and love Him. Through reason we know God and the world. Through Revelation, we know God in a deeper way, orienting all our actions toward him. The joy we experience in loving God is a hint of greater things to come. Someday, we hope, we will enjoy the ultimate Revelation. We will see God face-to-face in the company of the angels and saints, including, we hope and pray, our relatives and friends.

Endnotes

1 *CCC*, no. 52, citing *1 Timothy* 6:16 and *Ephesians* 1:4–5.

2 *CCC*, no. 85.

3 Vatican II, *Dei Verbum* (Dogmatic Constitution on Divine Revelation), no. 9; *CCC*, no. 81.

4 *CCC*, no. 81, quoting *Dei Verbum*, no. 9.

5 *Dei Verbum*, no. 7.

6 *CCC*, no. 83.

7 Patricia Keefe, "Blessed Miguel Pro," *Position Paper* 330/31 (June/July 2001): 195, 198.

8 Dwight P. Campbell, "St. Maximilian Kolbe and the Immaculate Conception," *Homiletic & Pastoral Review* (March 2005),:21; Lawrence Elliott, "The Heroism of Father Kolbe," *Reader's Digest* (July 1973): 2.

9 Brother Francis Mary, F.I., "Maximilian Kolbe, Saint for Our Times," http://www.wandererforum.org/essays/Mary.html/; see also, "Priest Hero of a Death Camp," http://www.catholic-pages.com/Saints/stmaximilian.asp/.

3. BUT CAN I *REALLY* KNOW ANYTHING?

"Apart from sense impressions, can I be absolutely sure of anything?" "No." "Are you absolutely sure of that?" "Yes."

In over four decades of teaching, from junior high to graduate law school, the author has often participated – as the questioner – in such an exchange. Nor are such answers always confined to the students' side of the room. If you go to college, whether "Catholic" or otherwise, you will sooner or later (and probably sooner) encounter professors who say that they cannot really know anything. Why you should pay tuition to "learn" from them is another question.

We are not concerned here with the normal reliability of sense impressions (what we see, hear, etc.), which we accept. Clearly, only a fool, or an academic, would ask for "proof" that the speeding truck he sees headed for him is really there. If he distrusts the evidence of his senses and does not jump out of the way, he will be a former academic. We are concerned here not about the reliability of sense impressions, but whether we can know anything beyond them. The answer is: Yes, we can.[1]

What is the first thing I can know?

Saint Thomas Aquinas distinguished the "speculative reason" from the "practical reason." This does not mean that our reason is divided into two parts. Rather, Saint Thomas was describing two aspects or operations of human reason. Reason has an "object," what it seeks to know and understand. When we use our reason to know the good, we call that the practical reason, which is discussed in depth later. When we use our reason to know the essence of a thing (what it is), we call that the speculative reason. We use the speculative reason to know the truth about something, and ultimately to know about being itself.[2]

The first principle, or rule, of the speculative reason is the principle of non-contradiction (or we can call it the principle of contradiction): A thing cannot be and not be at the same time under the same aspect. Another way of saying it is that the same thing cannot be affirmed and denied at the same time. This pen I am holding in my hand is a pen. Can it be at the same time

 something else? I could take it outside and dig a little trench with it, in which case it would be a shovel. Or I could lay it across that little trench so ants could walk across it, in which case it would be a bridge. The pen is also black, hard, cylindrical, five inches long, etc. But each of these involves considering the pen in an aspect different from its pen-ness. I know with absolute certainty that, in terms of its pen-ness, its being or not being a pen, it cannot be both a pen and not a pen. It is either a pen or not a pen. It is what it is – a pen. Being cannot be non-being. This is self-evident. Anyone who thinks that this item, in terms of its pen-ness, is both a pen and not a pen, is unfit to carry on a conversation. And if I ask for proof, if I say, "Prove that this cannot be, at the same time, both a pen and a wheelbarrow," the answer is that there is no proof and none is needed.

As a self-evident proposition, the principle of noncontradiction is known beyond doubt to all rational beings. The statement, "I cannot know anything," is itself absurd. For if I make that statement at least I claim to know that I cannot know anything. And if I say, "I just am not sure I can be sure of anything," I acknowledge at least that I am sure I am not sure. Or if I say, "I cannot know anything that cannot be verified by sense impression or by experimentation," I say something absurd because that statement itself cannot be verified by sense impression or by experimentation.

How do I know things?

Some people will deny even the principle of non-contradiction. They think, somehow, that being can be non-being, that the same thing can be affirmed and denied at the same time. Truth, however, is not determined by majority vote. Any rational person will acknowledge the truth of the principle of contradiction. The self-evident truth of that principle provides the first example of what we can know with certainty.

Beyond that, man is capable of knowing the essences or the natures of things. The essence of something is *what* it is, its substance or nature. We can know that this is a pen and not a battleship. Saint Thomas Aquinas teaches that our intellect has two faculties or abilities, which he calls the active intellect and the passive intellect. Man understands essences through the operation of his senses and his intellect. We perceive individual things through our external senses (sight, hearing, touch, taste, and smell), and our internal senses (imagination, memory, instinct, and common sense [which unifies and integrates in an orderly way the data provided by the senses]).

For example, my senses perceive Casey, the Farnan family dog. They present information to my mind. My mind then makes that information understandable and stores it. I can draw an analogy between the way the human mind works and the way computers work. (This is not surprising, for computers are modeled after the human mind.) Computers have two main functions: processing information (including solving problems) and storing information. The human mind, or intellect, similarly has two main powers. It processes information – it takes the sense impressions, that information presented to it by the senses, and abstracts from it the concept or idea of the object that I know. (Abstraction is explained some more in the next chapter.) This is called the active intellect.

Saint Thomas describes three acts of the intellect – three basic things that the intellect does. The first act of the intellect is *understanding*, which means the formation of an idea by which we know what kind of thing something is.[3] For example, as I look at the dog, Casey, I understand that she is a furry, four-legged creature that barks. The second act of the intellect is *judgment*: "That object is a dog," or, "This object is not a dog." A judgment will be true if it conforms to reality and false if it does not conform to reality. If I say that an airplane is a dog, my judgment is false; I know it is false because I know the nature of a dog and of an airplane. The third act of the intellect is *reasoning*, when I intellectually proceed from one thing that I know to another. I reason when I think logically, using what is known in philosophy as a syllogism, with a major premise ("All dogs are mortal."), minor premise ("Casey is a dog."), and conclusion ("Therefore, Casey is mortal."). Reasoning also includes solving problems, creating arguments, telling stories – any time my mind proceeds from one thought to another.

But our minds also receive and store the information that they have processed. Just as we can store information in a computer and use it again later, our minds have the power to store information for later use. This is called the passive intellect, and it includes memory. This does not mean that we have two intellects, though. We each have one intellect, and it has the power to work either actively or passively, just as one computer can both process and store information.

The computer analogy can help us understand how our minds work actively, but it doesn't do justice to the creativity and depth of the human spirit. "The human person participates in the light and power of the divine Spirit. By his reason, he is capable of understanding the order of things established by the Creator. By free will, he is capable of directing himself toward his true good."[4] A human person cannot be equated to, or placed on the same leveal as, a computer. Computers are mechanical, but human intellect is spiritual, with the ability to think creatively by creating stories and poetry, and the ability to invent novel ways to solve old problems. Human intellect is able to engage in abstract thought about ideas like beauty, truth and goodness. Our ability to think in an abstract way culminates in our ability to think about "the idea of being, which includes God, the only self-existent Being. 'I am who am.'"[5]

What's the idea?

Through our senses and intellects, therefore, we know the essence of a dog. French philosopher René Descartes (1596–1650) taught that an idea is that *which* we know; we can know only our own ideas and nothing else; therefore, if I say that Casey is an airplane rather than a dog, no one can say that I am wrong because no one can *know* what a dog or an airplane really is. Contrary to Descartes, an idea is not that *which* we know. Rather, an idea is that *by which* we know reality.[6]

The point of this chapter is that, apart from sense impressions, the mind can attain to knowledge of the world that is certain. Now we have to ask what we can know, especially about ourselves and about God.

Endnotes

1   See generally, Rice, *50 Questions on the Natural Law*, 125–39.
2   See Heinrich Rommen, *The Natural Law* (Indianapolis, Ind.: Liberty Fund, 1998), 141–47.
3   See *ST*, I, Q. 79; I Q. 84.
4   *CCC*, no. 1704.

5 Cornelius Hagerty, C.S.C., *The Problem of Evil* (Quincy, Mass.: Christopher Publishing House, 1978), 18.

6 See Pope John Paul II, *Crossing the Threshold of Hope* (New York: Knopf, 1995), 38, 51–52, discussing Descartes and Aquinas.

4. WHAT CAN I KNOW ABOUT MYSELF? CAN I *KNOW* WHETHER I WILL LIVE FOREVER?

The first point I need to know is that there are two types of reality: the material and the spiritual. A material thing, like a baseball, is composed of tangible parts. I can pick it up, hold it, and throw it. A spiritual thing is called "simple" because it has no parts, no shape, no size. I cannot hold it or touch it. But a spiritual being is just as real as a material one. The existence of spiritual reality – of real, spiritual beings – is not well understood today. But it is easy to prove.

What can I know about myself?[1]
Do I have a soul?

Yes. A soul is the life principle of a living thing. Every living thing – dog, tree, or housefly – has a soul. But the soul of a dog is not spiritual. We know this by observing that the dog or other animal never appears to perform the intellectual acts that only a spiritual being can perform. Its knowledge, memories, and desires are all sensory-based. When a beaver builds a dam, it does not read and follow plans it has devised; rather it acts by the instinct built into that beaver by its intelligent Maker. Have you ever seen a couple of birds standing on a branch, examining blueprints for a nest? No, and don't hold your breath waiting for it. Revelation confirms the fact, which we know by observation, that animals, insects, etc., differ from man in that they are wholly material.

Is my soul a spirit?

The soul of a dog is not material in the sense that we can see it or measure it. It is material in that its existence depends on the physical matter that is the dog. It is not of itself spiritual. When the dog dies, its soul goes out of existence. That is the nature of a material soul. Of course, God could choose to keep that dog alive for all eternity. We know that we, on the other hand, will be perfectly happy in heaven. A little boy once asked the wise priest, "Will I have my dog in heaven?," and the priest answered him: "If you want your dog in heaven you will have your dog in heaven." (Of course, in heaven I won't need anything besides God to be happy.) Of its nature, however, the dog's soul is not a spirit and is therefore not immortal.

But we are compounds – a material body and a spiritual soul – in living unity. How do we know that the human soul is spiritual? Because we can do two things that a merely material being cannot do. We can form abstract ideas and we can reflect on ourselves.

Abstraction

A baseball and an orange are both round. But "roundness" does not exist, by itself, in the material world. Yet we can think of "roundness" apart from any particular round thing. The idea, "roundness," is an abstract idea. We will never find "roundness" by itself in the material world. I can put a round ball in my gym bag, but I cannot put "roundness" there. We can think about "roundness" without visualizing any specific round thing. When we think of "roundness" we are not merely registering sense impressions. We are abstracting from our sense impressions a concept, "roundness," which does not exist of itself in the material world apart from a material, round thing. Other examples of abstract ideas are "truth," "honesty," "love," etc.

Every time we use a common noun we perform the spiritual

act of abstraction. We know that what we are reading is a book because it has the abstract quality of "bookness," that which makes it a book. Books may differ in size, shape, color, etc., but we know the difference between a book and a rock because we have the abstract ideas of "bookness" and "rockness." We know the essence (what it is) of a book and of a rock. If we call a book a rock, our statement is false because it does not conform to the reality that the item we are naming has the abstract qualities of "bookness" and does not have the abstract qualities of "rockness." So every time we use a common noun to identify something – "this is a cup" – we give evidence that we are spiritual.

Our ability to design things also illustrates our capacity for abstraction. Suppose I am going to build a birdhouse. The first thing I will do is visualize it as I want to build it, with a sauna, an escalator, a putting green, etc. When I visualize that birdhouse, I am forming an abstract idea of something that does not yet exist in the material world. My concept of the birdhouse, or of the book I want to write, is an abstract idea. Birds do not design their houses. They build them according to the instinct built into them by their intelligent Designer. But my design of the birdhouse is a spiritual activity, different in kind from mere registration of sense impressions. Incidentally, the fact that God designed us and the universe is one of the proofs that God is spiritual, since designing is a spiritual activity.[2]

Reflection

In addition to our ability to form abstract ideas, our ability to reflect on ourselves is the second ability that proves we are spiritual. We know that we can think about our entire self, our thoughts, our life history, etc. We have the ability to look at our whole self; we can, in a sense, get outside of ourselves and look back on ourselves. We can even reflect on the fact that we are reflecting. A material thing cannot get outside of itself and look back on itself. If we take a piece of paper and fold it over, the top half can look at the bottom half and the bottom half can look at the top half. But because the paper is matter and is limited by its material dimensions, it cannot get outside of itself and look back on its entire self. Only a spiritual thing can reflect upon itself. The fact that we can do it proves that we are spiritual. So – we know that our soul is spiritual. But why is that a big deal? Because it means that we will never go out of existence.[3]

Can I be sure that I will live forever?

Yes.[4] We know that our soul is spiritual because we can do spiritual things, that is, we can abstract and reflect. A spiritual being is, by its nature, immortal, that is, it will never die. Of course, God has the power to annihilate any created thing, including our souls, but He has given us His word in Revelation that He will not do that. The point in this chapter is that, of its very nature, our souls are immortal.

The death of anything occurs when it breaks up into its component parts. In a way, graduation signals the "death" of the unit that was a basketball team. Upon graduation the members go their separate ways. The death of a human being is the separation of the component parts of that human being – the body and the soul – a material part and a spiritual part which itself has no parts.

The death of a human being occurs when the soul leaves the body. The determination of whether death has occurred in a particular case is a scientific, rather than a theological, question. Apart from sudden, traumatic deaths, people generally die in stages. The first stage is clinical death, the cessation of spontaneous respiration and circulation; the lungs and heart stop working. This used to be conclusive evidence of death, but science is developing more sophisticated but debatable criteria, including what is loosely called "brain death." Once the applicable medical criteria are satisfied to permit the conclusion that the patient is dead, that is, that his soul has left the body, the patient's organs can be removed for transplanting to another person. Of course, an unpaired organ such as a heart, cannot morally be removed from a donor who is alive. That would be homicide. "[I]t is not morally admissible directly to bring about the disabling mutilation or death of a human being, even in order to delay the death of other persons."⁵

After the death of the human being, which occurs when the soul and body have separated, the third stage of death occurs. This is cellular death or the death of the body, in which the body decomposes, separating into its component parts.

The death of anything is its breaking up into its component parts. But the human soul, being spiritual, has no parts and therefore, of its nature, it will not die. As the noted Catholic writer, Father Leo Trese, summarized it:

> If the soul is a spirit, it must than be immortal, incapable of death. Because by definition a spirit is a simple substance, with no parts, no extension in space. (Part of my soul is not in my head, and part in my hands, and part in my feet. All of my soul is in every part of me, much as all of God is in every part of the Universe.)
>
> The soul being a simple substance, independent of the limitations of matter, it follows that there is nothing in the soul that can decompose, be destroyed, or cease to be. Death is the breaking up of a living organism into its component parts; but with the human soul, there just isn't anything "to break up." Thus our reason alone, even aside from God's divine revelation, tells us that our soul will never die.⁶

When Fr. Trese describes the soul as a simple substance he means it has no parts and no material dimensions. We already know from reason that this is so because our souls can form abstract ideas and can reflect on themselves, actions which no material being can do.

A day will come when we will die. Our bodies will then die and decompose. But our souls will never die. "Every man receives his eternal recompense in his immortal soul from the moment of his death in a particular judgment by Christ."⁷ In that judgment he will receive "either entrance into . . . heaven – through a purification or immediately, – or immediate and everlasting damnation."[8] Divine Revelation teaches that our bodies will be reunited with our souls at the Last Judgment. We will live on for all eternity, whether we want to or not. "Our justification," and therefore our chance for heaven, "comes from the grace of God . . . the *free and undeserved help* that God gives us to respond to his call to become children of God, adoptive sons, partakers of the divine nature and of eternal life."[9] The place of our eternal residence, heaven or hell, depends on our response to his call. To say the least, the realization of this should affect the way we live.

.

Endnotes

1 See generally *ST*, I, Q. 75–102.

2 James H. Dolan, s.j., *Theses in Natural Theology* (Ann Arbor, Mich.: Edwards, 1952), 29.

3 Rice, *50 Questions on the Natural Law*, 143–46.

4 See *ST*, I, Q. 75, art. 6; see also Rice, *50 Questions on the Natural Law*, 146–49.

5 *CCC*, no. 2296. For a discussion of problems raised by the use of brain death criteria to justify removal of unpaired and other organs, see Bishop Fabian Bruskewitz, et al, "Are Organ Transplants *Ever* Morally Licit?" *Catholic World Report* (March 2001): 53.

6 Leo J. Trese, *Wisdom Shall Enter* (Notre Dame, Ind.: Fides, 1964), 29–30.

7 *CCC*, no. 1051.

8 *CCC*, no. 1022, citing Council of Lyons II (1274); Denzinger 857–58, 990, 1000–1002, 1820; Council of Florence (1439); Council of Trent (1563); Benedict XII, *Benedictus Deus* (1336); and John XXII, *Ne super his* (1334).

9 *CCC*, no. 1996, citing *John* 1:12–18, 17:3; *Romans* 8:14–17; and *2 Peter* 1:3–4.

5. WHAT CAN I KNOW ABOUT GOD? CAN I *KNOW* THAT GOD EVEN EXISTS?

"Make a note of the difference there is between believing in the existence of God and believing in him."[1] It is not enough merely to believe that God exists. The fallen angels, the devils, know that God exists. My objective is to believe in God, to believe in him not as some kind of force but as my personal, loving Creator. I can remove obstacles to making that act of faith if I consider the evidence that shows that belief in God is the only reasonable conclusion.

> In . . . his Letter to the Romans, St. Paul . . . declares
> a profound truth: through all that is created the "eyes of
> the mind" can come to know God. Through the medium
> of creatures, God stirs in reason an intuition of his
> "power" and his "divinity." . . . [B]y discoursing on the
> data provided by the senses, reason can reach the cause
> which lies at the origin of all perceptible reality. . . . [I]t
> was part of the original plan of the creation that reason
> should without difficulty reach beyond the sensory data
> to the origin of all things: the Creator. But because of
> the disobedience by which man and woman chose to set
> themselves in full and absolute autonomy in relation to
> the One who had created them, this ready access to God
> the Creator diminished.[2]

Through faith we know that God exists. Is that merely a blind faith unsupported by reason? What, if anything, can reason tell us about God? In his encyclical, *Faith and Reason*, John Paul II said, "Faith and reason are like two wings on which the human spirit rises to the contemplation of truth."[3] Reason, obviously, cannot provide us with complete knowledge of the infinite God. But, as the Second Vatican Council affirmed, "God, the beginning and end of all things, can be known with certainty from created reality by the light of human reason."[4] As the defeated French emperor, Napoleon Bonaparte, stood on the deck of the ship transporting him to his last prison at St. Helena, he is said to have pointed up to the stars and remarked, "Say what you please, someone created and controls all that."[5]

Saint Thomas Aquinas (1225–1274) gave us five ways from reason to prove the existence of God.[6] The first three proofs depend on *the self-evident principle of sufficient reason: that nothing can exist without a sufficient reason for its existence and that every effect must have a cause.* If I were holding a pen in my hand and dropped it onto the desk and you asked me, "Why did the pen drop?" I would say, "Because I opened my fingers, because I sent a message from my brain to do so, and because the law of gravity then took over." But if you asked, "Why did the pen drop?" and I said, "No reason," would you believe it? Of course not. Everyone knows that the principle of sufficient reason is true, and Aquinas uses it to show the existence of God. Here are the five proofs:[7]

1. *Motion.* If I stopped at the railroad crossing and saw a freight car go by, all by itself, I would be surprised and think,

"How is it moving?" I would look for a source of that movement. What is in motion must have been put in motion by another and that mover must itself have been put in motion by another again. This process cannot go on to infinity. Therefore, there must be a first mover in the series that is itself unmoved and that is the source of all movement. This prime mover is God.

2. *Causation.* This proof also depends on the principles that nothing can exist without a sufficient reason and that every effect must have a cause. A thing cannot be the cause of itself. If it were, it would have to have existed prior to itself, which is impossible. Every effect must have a cause, but that cause in turn must be the effect of another cause, and so on. But the process cannot go on to infinity. There must be a first cause of it all that is not caused and that has in itself the sufficient reason for its existence. That uncaused first cause is God.

3. *Necessity or contingency.* According to the self-evident principle of sufficient reason, anything that exists must have a sufficient reason for its existence. How do we know that there always had to be an eternal being in existence, a being that had no beginning? We know that because the alternative is to say that there was a time when there was absolutely nothing in existence. But when we think about it, if there was ever a time when there was nothing, there could never be anything. From nothing, nothing can come. As Julie Andrews put it in the film version of *The Sound of Music*, "Nothing comes from nothing. Nothing ever could." To explain the existence of beings that at one time did not exist, there must have always existed a necessary being, from whom beings that began to be received their existence. The existence of all other beings is contingent; it depends on the existence of this necessary being. *Why is there something rather than nothing?* Because there always was, and is, an eternal Being. This necessary, eternal Being is God.

4. *Perfection.* Building on the third proof, in which he makes the case that nothing comes from nothing, Saint Thomas points out that there must be an ultimate source of all that is good, including existence itself. When we look at things, statements, or

people, we can judge that they are more or less good, beautiful, true, etc. We can judge that they possess various perfections. The most basic of these perfections, and one that everything possesses, is existence or being itself, for we cannot have any other perfection unless we exist. Because nothing comes from nothing, there must be an absolute source of all perfection, the most perfect being, from which less perfect beings derive all of their perfections, but especially their existence. Therefore there must also be something which is to all beings the cause of their being, goodness and every other perfection; and this we call God. While the third proof tells us that all existence comes from God, this proof tells us that all that is good, including all perfections and especially existence, comes from God.

5. *Design.* If someone told me that he got his watch by buying all the parts, putting them in a bag, shaking the bag and then reaching into the bag and pulling out the watch, would I believe it? Of course not. The watch was obviously designed by an intelligent designer. How much more so with the human body, the world and the universe. Is it theoretically possible for the human brain to be the product of chance or some blind force of necessity? Yes, in theory, but do we really believe it happened that way? Suppose I was walking on the beach and saw traced in the sand these letters: "NOTRE DAME. GO IRISH!" Would I say, "Oh look at the letters the waves made in the sand"? It is unreasonable to think that those letters were anything but the work of an intelligent designer. So it is with the world. It is unreasonable to conclude that the world is anything but the purposeful work of an intelligent designer. That designer is God. "Science must recognize," said John Paul II, "its inability to reach the existence of God: it can neither affirm nor deny his existence. . . . However, we must not [conclude] that scientists . . . are unable to find valid reasons for admitting the existence of God. . . . [T]he scientist . . . can discover in the world reasons for affirming a Being which surpasses it."[8] "[M]an is capable of knowing God by reason alone . . . even though indirectly and not immediately," concluded John Paul II.[9]

Whittaker Chambers, a member of a Communist spy ring in the United States during the 1930s, dated his break from Communism to "a very casual happening. I was sitting in my apartment . . . in Baltimore . . . . My daughter was in her high chair. I was watching her eat. . . . My eye came to rest on the delicate convolutions of her ear – those intricate, perfect ears. The thought passed through my mind: 'No, those ears were not created by any chance coming together of atoms in nature (the Communist view). They could have been created only by immense design.' The thought was involuntary and unwanted. . . . But I never wholly forgot it. . . . I had to crowd it out of my mind. If I had completed it, I should have had to say: Design presupposes God. I did not then know that, at that moment, the finger of God was first laid upon my forehead."[10]

In addition to these five proofs of Saint Thomas Aquinas, two other proofs for the existence of God are relevant:

The Argument from Conscience. The nineteenth-century English Cardinal, John Henry Newman explained this:

> If, as is the case, we feel responsibility, are ashamed, are frightened, at transgressing the voice of conscience, this implies that there is One to whom we are responsible, before whom we are ashamed, whose claims upon us we fear. If, on doing wrong, we feel the same tearful, broken-hearted sorrow which overwhelms us in hurting a mother; if, on doing right, we enjoy the same sunny serenity of mind, the same soothing, satisfactory delight which follows on our receiving praise from a father, we certainly have within us the image of some person, to whom our love and veneration look, in whose smile we find our happiness, for whom we yearn, towards whom we direct our pleadings, in whose anger we are troubled and waste away. These feelings in us are such as require for their exciting cause an intelligent Being; we are not affectionate towards a stone, nor do we feel shame

before a horse or a dog; we have no remorse or compunction on breaking mere human law; yet, so it is, conscience excites all these painful emotions, confusion, foreboding, self-condemnation; and on the other hand it sheds upon us a deep peace, a sense of security, a resignation and a hope, which there is no sensible, no earthly object to elicit. "The wicked flees when no one pursueth;" then why does he flee? whence his terror? Who is it that he sees in solitude, in darkness, in the hidden chambers of his heart? If the cause of these emotions does not belong to this visible world, the Object to which his perception is directed must be Supernatural and Divine; and thus the phenomena of Conscience, as a dictate, avail to impress the imagination with the picture of a Supreme Governor, a Judge, holy, just, powerful, all-seeing, retributive, and is the creative principle of religion, as the Moral Sense is the principle of ethics.[11]

The Argument from Universal Belief. "Throughout history," declared the Second Vatican Council, "there is found among different peoples a certain awareness of a hidden power, which lies behind the course of nature and the events of human life. At times there is present even a recognition of a supreme Being, or still more of a Father."[12] Every people, race or tribe, with few exceptions, has had some kind of belief in a higher power or Being, despite wide variances in those beliefs. The existence of such a practically universal belief supports the conclusion that something real explains that belief. Such a belief, among men of all times and cultures, cannot reasonably be accounted for except on the basis that it is a right conclusion of human reason. Its universality is evidence of its reasonableness. This does not mean that truth is determined by consensus or majority vote. But the persistence of belief in God among peoples of all times and places indicates that there is something to that belief.

It is unreasonable not to believe in God

We often tend to be apologetic, and assume that our religion is a blind leap of faith and that the atheists are the reasonable people. Rather, belief in God is fully reasonable. In fact, it is wholly unreasonable not to believe in God. To deny that God exists we must be prepared to say that an endless chain of movers is possible without an unmoved first mover; that an infinite chain of causes is conceivable without an uncaused first cause; that something can come from absolutely nothing; that there is no ultimate cause of all that is good, including existence; that the workings of the human body and of the universe can occur through chance without intelligent design; and that the universal testimony of man through the ages and of the human conscience is of no account.

"The fool," said John Paul II, "thinks that he knows many things, but really he is incapable of fixing his gaze on the things that truly matter. . . . And so when he claims that 'God does not exist' . . . he shows with absolute clarity just how deficient his knowledge is and just how far he is from the full truth of things, their origin and their destiny."[13]

Endnotes

1 Saint John Vianney, *Thoughts of the Cure D'Ars* (Rockford, Ill.: TAN Books, 1984), 50.

2 *FR*, no. 22; see ST, I, Q. 88, art. 3.

3 *FR*, Preamble.

4 Vatican II, *Lumen Gentium*, no. 6.

5 Henry J. Taylor, "Unquenchable Flame of Faith," *New York World-Telegram Sun* (Nov. 25, 1964).

6 See Rice, *50 Questions on the Natural Law*, 153–62.

7 *ST*, I, Q. 2, art. 3.

8 Pope John Paul II, Audience, July 10, 1985; *The Wanderer* (Aug. 8, 1985): 1.

9 Pope John Paul II, Audience, Mar. 20, 1985; *The Wanderer* (April 11, 1985): 1.

10 Whittaker Chambers, "A Letter to my Children," in *President's Essay* (Washington, D.C.: Heritage Foundation, 1986), 20.

11 John Henry Cardinal Newman, *Grammar of Assent*, ch. 5, sec. 1 (Garden City, N.Y.: Doubleday, 1955), 101.

12 Vatican II, *Nostra Aetate* (*Declaration on the Relationship of the Church to Non-Christian Religions*).

13 *FR*, no. 18.

6. CAN I *KNOW* WHAT GOD IS LIKE?

So I think there is a God. But do I know anything about him? Is there only one? Why not two Gods? Can God do everything? Can he make a rock so heavy that he can't lift it? Can he make mistakes? Does he know everything? Does he know that I am going to steal that car tomorrow? If he does, why doesn't he stop me? If he knows in advance that I am going to steal the car, how can it be my free decision to steal it? And so on.

Can reason tell me anything about God?

The first step in answering these questions is to reassure ourselves, as noted in the previous chapter, "that man *is capable* of knowing God by reason alone: he is capable of a *certain 'knowledge' about God*, even though indirectly and not immediately."[1] This ability of reason to know God is a settled, dogmatic teaching of the Church. The First Vatican Council (1869–1870) stated: "Holy Mother Church holds and teaches that God, the origin and end of all things, can be known with certainty by the natural light of human reason from the things that he created."[2] That Council went on to describe God:

> The holy, Catholic, apostolic Roman Church believes and professes that there is one true and living God, the Creator and Lord of heaven and earth. He is almighty, eternal, beyond measure, incomprehensible, and infinite

in intellect, will and in every perfection. Since he is one unique spiritual substance, entirely simple and unchangeable, he must be declared really and essentially distinct from the world, perfectly happy in himself and by his very nature, and inexpressibly exalted over all things that exist or can be conceived other than himself.[3]

So what is God like?

We can know from reason that God is:

1. *One.* It is impossible that there could be more than one necessary and infinite uncaused first cause. If there were two or three "gods," someone higher up (Supergod?) must have caused *them*. Saint Thomas points out that if there were more than one God, there would have to be differences between them, that is, they would possess different perfections. But if there were differences between them, then each one would lack some kind of perfection that the other one had. Suppose, for example, that the first god was all-knowing (but not almighty), while the second god was almighty (but not all-knowing). Neither of these two gods would be absolutely perfect. We know from the proofs for the existence of God that God, the cause of all perfections, is absolutely perfect. So there must be only one God.[4]

2. *Infinite,* or without limit. God is the one necessary, self-sufficient Being, the cause of all other beings. He is all-perfect. As Fr. John Hardon put it, "the Fathers of the Church . . . speak of God as infinite, boundless, uncircumscribed. . . . [T]his goes beyond affirming that God has no limitations. It says that he has within himself the fullness of all perfection, whether knowledge or power or being."[5]

3. *Simple.* This means that God has no parts. If God did have parts, who made the parts and who put them together? (Supergod again?) If we are looking at a being with parts, we can be sure we are not looking at God. Aquinas explains, as summarized by Monsignor Glenn:

Since God is infinite and uncaused, it follows that he is *simple*, i.e., not composed of parts or elements. In other words, God is not a *composite* or *compounded* being. Every composite being is contingent upon the union of its parts and requires a uniting cause to bring these parts into union. . . . Again, the parts of a composite being are logically or naturally prior to their union; and there is nothing prior to the eternal God, the *necessary* First Cause. God, therefore, is *simple*. He has *no possessed parts or perfections*; His perfections are one with His undivided essence; all that God *has*, *He is*. Thus . . . God does not *have* wisdom; God *is* Wisdom. . . . Similarly, God is Infinite Justice, Infinite Mercy, Infinite Power, etc.[6]

4. **Spiritual.** "Since God is simple, He is spiritual. For a real . . . being must be either bodily or spiritual. Now, a bodily being is always made of bodily parts . . . and . . . is composite. But, as we have seen, God is not composite, but simple. He is therefore not bodily; it remains that He is spiritual."[7]

5. **Eternal.** As the necessary Being, God must be eternal, which means that he always was and always will be. If there was ever a time when there was nothing, there could never be anything. "The proof of God's eternity lies in the fact of His necessity. A necessary being must exist, and cannot be non-existent; existence belongs to its very essence. Obviously such a being is *always* a necessary being ([or] else, it *began* to be necessary under action of some cause, and so is *contingent* and not necessary at all!); and being always necessary, it is always existent; in other words, it is *eternal*."[8]

6. **Personal.** A person is an individual with intellect and will. God designed and created the world, which he could not have done if he did not have intellect and will. Designing, as shown in Chapter 4, is a spiritual act of the intellect and can only be done by a person. "The intelligence of the First

Cause of the universe can be deduced from the fact that in the universe there are intelligent beings; no effect can be essentially superior to its efficient cause. However, a more detailed and satisfying argument can be developed in the so-called teleological proof; there is a constant and universal manifestation of order in the world, an order characterized by such purposeful activity and harmonious design that it must be according to the plan  of an intelligent designer. . . . The order and harmony and design of the world as a whole, as a complete thing, can never be adequately accounted for unless I admit that the ultimate efficient cause of that universe is intelligent."[9]

7. **Omnipresent.** All of God is everywhere because he is infinite, the necessary first cause. As a spirit, God is not present in a place in the same way that a material object is present. "God is wholly and entirely present in every place, and . . . He is not circumscribed or bounded by the boundaries of the place. God is wholly present in all the world. . . . But he is in no wise identified with the world – the proof of this lies in God's infinity. For the infinite must have limitless perfection – including the perfection of existence everywhere – and must be free from every limitation – such as being bounded or constrained within the limits of any place or places."[10]

8. **Omniscient.** *Do we really have free will?* "God knows everything, past, present, and future. Nothing has happened, is now happening, or will or could happen in the future that is not dependent on the infinite power of the necessary being who is God. And God is not subject to the limitations of time.

God knows whether we shall go to Chicago next year, whether we shall succeed in school, and whether we shall sin.

'If there could be anything, actual or possible, hidden from God's knowledge, then God would not be infinite; He would be limited by the limitation of His knowledge.'"[11] "However, God's knowledge (or foreknowledge) of what we do does not deprive us of free will in doing it. . . . [W]e distinguish God's will from his knowledge. But his knowledge of what we will do is not causative; His knowledge does not force us to do anything nor does it predetermine our acts, although he knows what we will choose to do."[12] Our limited human intellect cannot understand *how* God's foreknowledge can coexist with our freedom of will. But we know *that* they *do* coexist. God, of course, has infinite knowledge, including knowledge of the future. And common human experience confirms that we *do* have freedom of will:

> *The human will in many actions enjoys a true freedom of choice* . . . . In many of our acts we have this clear consciousness of our freedom of choice: (1) *Before the act*, we are conscious of our deliberation about the reasons for or against a definite action; without freedom of choice, this deliberation would be absurd. (2) *During the decision*, we are conscious of free consent, and because of this we are careful, realizing we are assuming responsibility. (3) *After the decision*, we are conscious that we could have decided otherwise, and we blame or praise ourselves alone for any regret or credit accruing from the action. Unless our wills had a freedom of choice with regard to these actions, the deliberation, decision, and assumption of merit or demerit would be absurd.[13]

"The simple words 'Thank you,'" said Archbishop Fulton J. Sheen, "will always stand out as a refutation of determinism, for they imply that something which was done could possibly have been left undone."[14]

9. **Omnipotent.** There is nothing that God, the all-powerful and infinite Being, cannot do. Could God make a rock so heavy he could not lift it? Or make a square circle? These are contradictions; they cannot exist or even be conceived to exist. They are no-thing. "To say that God is omnipotent is to say that He is *almighty*. . . . God does not make any *effort* in accomplishing what He wills to do, nor is He limited to one work at a time, nor is He fatigued by His work, nor is His work built up, so to speak, bit by bit. God perfectly accomplishes what He wills to do by the eternal decrees of His perfect *will*. With God, to will and to perform is one and the same act. The proof of these assertions is found in God's infinite perfection. Infinite perfection includes boundless power, and excludes the imperfections of toil, effort, fatigue, successive partial accomplishment, etc."[15]

10. **All-perfect.** God, the infinite Being, has the fullness of all perfections. God does not merely possess perfections. Rather he is perfection in his very nature. Therefore, God is goodness, God is love, God is wisdom, etc.

Reason can tell us quite a lot about God. But God did not leave us dependent on reason alone. Chapter 7 tells us what God has told us about himself that we could not know from our reason.

Endnotes

1 Pope John Paul II, *Audience,* Mar. 20, 1985; *The Wanderer* (Apr. 11, 1985), 1.

2 First Vatican Council, *Dogmatic Constitution on the Catholic Faith*, no. 2.

3 *Ibid.*, no. 1; John A. Hardon, S.J., *The Catholic Catechism* (Garden City, N.Y.: Doubleday, 1981), 55.

4 See Paul J. Glenn, *A Tour of the Summa*, (Rockford, Ill.: TAN Books, 1978), 12.

5   John A. Hardon, S.J., *The Catholic Catechism*, (Doubleday, 1981), 56–57.

6   Paul J. Glenn, *Apologetics* (TAN Books, 1980), 59–60.

7   *Ibid.*, 60.

8   *Ibid.*, 65.

9   James H. Dolan, S.J., *Theses in Natural Theology* (Ann Arbor, Mich.: Edwards, Ann Arbor, 1952), 29.

10   Paul J. Glenn, *Apologetics*, 66.

11   *Ibid.* 67.

12   Charles E. Rice, *50 Questions on the Natural Law* (San Francisco: Ignatius, 1999), 168–69.

13   Joseph F. Sullivan, S.J., *General Ethics* (Worcester, Mass.: Holy Cross College Press, 1948), 3 (Emphasis added).

14   Fulton J. Sheen, *The Life of All Living* (New York: The Century Co., 1929), 15.

15   Paul J. Glenn, *Apologetics*, 68–69.

7. WHAT HAS GOD TOLD ME ABOUT HIMSELF? WHAT DOES HE DO FOR A LIVING?

I know from reason that God is personal. But God has told me that he is not just one person. When he created, God said, "Let *us* make man to *our* image and likeness." But then *Genesis* says, "And God created man to *his* own image and likeness; to the image of God he created him."[1] "I and the Father are One," said Christ.[2] "Go, therefore, and make disciples of all nations, baptizing them in *the name* of the Father, and of the Son, and of the Holy Spirit."[3]

How can three persons have one name? "Christians are baptized," says the Catechism, "in the *name* of the Father and of the Son and of the Holy Spirit: not in their *names*, for there is only one God, the almighty Father, his only Son, and the Holy Spirit: the Most Holy Trinity."[4] The Trinity – one God in three divine persons – is a supernatural mystery, beyond my understanding but not inconsistent with reason. It is "the central mystery of Christian faith and life."[5]

What is the Trinity?

The early Councils of the Church defined some truths about the Trinity. "We do not confess three Gods, but one God in three persons. . . . The divine persons do not share the one divinity among themselves but each of them is God whole and entire . . . 'by nature one God.'"[6] Person refers to who I am. Nature refers to what I am. Who I am is John Smith. What I am is a human being; that is my nature. Each human person has one nature, which is human. In God there are three divine persons in the one divine nature. *"The divine persons are really distinct from one another."*[7] But there is one divine "'nature or substance.' . . . 'Because of that unity the Father is wholly in the Son and wholly in the Holy Spirit; the Son is wholly in the Father and wholly in the Holy Spirit; the Holy Spirit is wholly in the Father and wholly in the Son.'"[8] Because the three persons of the Trinity have the one divine nature, they "know with the same intellect and love with the same will."[9]

The three persons did not come into existence one after another. They did not "come into existence" at all. All three are eternal. As God, the Father existed from all eternity and his intellect and will operated from all eternity. The operation of my intellect produces an idea, a word, but the operation of the Father's intellect produced, from all eternity, not an idea but another person, the Son. Saint John's Gospel refers to the Second Person of the Trinity as "the Word."[10] "The First Person knows Himself; His act of knowing Himself produces an Idea, a Word; and this Idea, this Word, the perfect Image of Himself, is the Second Person."[11] From all eternity the relation of the Father and the Son is a relation of love, and that love produces from all eternity another person, the Holy Spirit. "We believe then in the Father who eternally begets the Son, in the Son, the Word of God, who is eternally begotten, in the Holy Spirit, the uncreated Person who proceeds from the Father and the Son as their eternal Love."[12]

In Chapter 6, we saw that we can know from reason that God does not merely possess perfections. He is perfection in his very nature. Thus, "God is love."[13] "God's very being," says the Catechism, "is love."[14] "By sending his only Son and the Spirit of Love . . . God has revealed his innermost secret: God himself is an eternal exchange of love, Father, Son and Holy Spirit, and he has destined us to share in that exchange."[15]

Love is an act of the will. "To love is to will the good of

another."[16] The wills of the eternal Father and the eternal Son operate from all eternity and from their love proceeds, from all eternity, another eternal person, the Holy Spirit. "God the Father is God, knowing himself. God the Son is the expression of God's knowledge of himself. God the Holy Spirit is the result of God's love for Himself."[17] The three persons of the Trinity have (or *are)* a social life. Theirs is a life of activity. It is a life of knowledge and love.

When we are commanded by God to love one another, it is a command to imitate the essential activity of the Trinity – for in loving one another we emulate the action of God himself. And we are "destined" to share in that life of love in perfect happiness forever. Provided, that is, that we don't mess it up by refusing it.

Endnotes

1 *Genesis* 1:26–27. (Emphasis added.)

2 *John* 10:30.

3 *Matthew* 28:19, New American Bible translation.

4 *CCC*, no. 233, citing Profession of faith of Pope Vigilius I (552).

5 *CCC*, no. 234.

6 *CCC*, no. 253, citing Council of Constantinople II (553) and quoting Council of Toledo XI (675).

7 *CCC*, no. 254.

8 *CCC*, no. 255, quoting Council of Toledo XI (675) and Council of Florence (1442).

9 Frank J. Sheed, *Theology and Sanity* (Huntington, Ind.: Our Sunday Visitor, 1978), 56.

10 *John* 1:1.

11 Frank J. Sheed, *Theology and Sanity*, 62.

12 Pope Paul VI, *The Credo of the People of God* (1968).

13 *1 John* 4:8, 16.

14 *CCC*, no. 221.

15 *Ibid.*, citing *1 Corinthians* 2:7–16, *Ephesians* 3:9–12.

16 *CCC*, no. 1766, quoting *ST* I-II, Q. 26, art. 4.

17 Leo Trese, *The Faith Explained* (Sinag-tala, Manila, 1991), 24.

8. WHY DID GOD MAKE *ME* – AND EVERYONE ELSE?

When God creates he makes something out of nothing. "God said, 'Let there be light,' and there was light. . . . Then God said, 'Let there be a firmament in the midst of the waters to divide the waters.' And so it was. . . . God created man in His image. In the image of God He created him. Male and female He created them."[1]

God created on three levels:

* the purely *spiritual* – the angels;
* the *material and spiritual* – man, who is composed of a material body and a spiritual soul; and
* the *material* – the rocks, trees, etc.

Angels were created first. They have no bodies. But they are persons, with intellect and will. "[T]he angels are *servants* and messengers of God."[2] God did not need to create the angels or anything else. He created angels out of his infinite love so that they could love him and share in the perfect and unending happiness of the life of the Trinity. But love is an act of the will. "When God made the angels, He made each with a will that was supremely free. I know that the price of heaven is love for God. It is by making an act of love for God that a spirit, whether an angel or a human soul, fits itself for heaven. The love must be proved in the only way in which love for God *can* be proved – by a free and voluntary submission of the created will to God, by what we commonly call an 'act of obedience' or an 'act of loyalty.' God made the angels with free wills so they might be capable of making their act of love, their choice of God. Only after they had done so would they see God face to face, only then would they enter into that everlasting union with God which we call 'heaven.'"³

Who committed the first sin?

To be able to love, one has to be a spirit with free will. Neither my ham sandwich nor my cat can love me, no matter how much I may say that I "love" each of them. The angels had Heaven open before them. All they had to do was choose to love God. Some of the angels rejected God. They refused to acknowledge God as God, and they refused to love and obey him. They said, to use the Latin, "Non serviam!" – "I will not serve!" This was the first sin. It was the beginning of Hell, which "is, essentially, the eternal separation of a spirit from Almighty God. Later on, when the human race would sin in the person of Adam, God would give the human race a second chance. But there was no second chance for the sinning angels. Because of the perfect clarity of their angelic minds and the unhampered freedom of their angelic wills, even the infinite mercy of God could find no excuse for the sin of the angels. They understood (to a degree that Adam never did) what the full consequence of their sin would be. With them there was no 'temptation,' in the sense in which we ordinarily understand the word. Theirs was what we would call a cold-blooded sin. By their deliberate and fully aware rejection of God, their wills were fixed against God, fixed forever. For them there was no turning back; they did not want to turn back. Their choice was made for eternity. There burns in them an everlasting hatred for God and all His works."⁴

The faithful angels, however, "have been present . . . throughout the history of salvation . . . serving . . . the divine plan."⁵ "The whole life of the Church benefits from the . . . help of angels."⁶ And "each believer" has a guardian angel "as protector and shepherd leading him to life."⁷

The first humans: were there really only two?

After the creation of the angels, God created the material world. And then he created man, for the same reason that he created the angels, so that man could choose to share in the social life of the Trinity in perfect happiness forever.

"God created man in his own image, in the image of God he created him, male and female he created them."[8] "Man occupies a unique place  in creation: (I) he is 'in the image of God'; (II) in his own nature he unites the spiritual and material worlds; (III) he is created 'male and female'; (IV) God established him in his friendship."[9]

> Of all visible creatures only man is "able to know and love his Creator." He is "the only creature on earth that God has willed for its own sake," and he alone is called to share, by knowledge and love, in God's own life. It was for this end that he was created, and this is the fundamental reason for his dignity.[10]

"[O]ur first parents, Adam and Eve, were constituted in an original 'state of holiness and justice.' This grace of original holiness was 'to share . . . in divine life.'"[11] They had a pretty good deal:

> By the radiance of this grace all dimensions of man's life were confirmed. As long as he remained in the divine intimacy, man would not have to suffer or die. The inner harmony of the human person, the harmony between man and woman, and finally the harmony

between the first couple and all creation, comprised the
state called "original justice." . . .

The sign of man's familiarity with God is that God
places him in the garden. There he lives "to till it and
keep it." Work is not yet a burden, but rather the collaboration of man and woman with God in perfecting the
visible creation.[12]

Was my ancestor a chimp?

"[T]he faithful cannot embrace that opinion which main-
tains either that after Adam there existed on this earth true men
who did not take their origin through natural generation from
him as from the first parent of all, or that Adam represents a certain number of first parents."[13] In other words, we are all related.
The next time some crazy driver cuts me off at an intersection,
I'll think about that. Before I say unkind things about his ances-
try, I have to remember that he is my distant relative. "[A]ll
human beings are one because they come from a single father,
Adam, and a single mother, Eve, 'the mother of all the living.'"[14]

How does this square with the theory of evolution, that man
has evolved from lower forms of life? This book is not the place
to analyze the many theories advanced in this area. The central
reality is that man is composed of a material body and a spiritual soul. In theory, God could have created matter in such a way
that the human body would evolve from lower forms and
species. Such evolution of the body has not been proved.
Evolution involves the development of parts. Whatever the scientific conjectures about evolution of the human body, the
human soul, because it is spiritual and has no parts, could not
evolve. God could have created matter so that it would evolve
into a human body. But God would have had to infuse the spiritual soul of man into that evolving matter. Only when the evolving matter was infused with a spiritual soul would man exist. If
the evolution of the body were ever proven, it would not disturb
our faith, for only the creative power of God could explain the

origin of matter and of the spiritual soul which could not evolve from matter. "The Church teaches that every spiritual soul is created immediately by God – it is not 'produced' by the parents – and also that it is immortal: it does not perish when it separates from the body at death, and it will be reunited with the body at the final Resurrection."[15]

In his 1996 address to the Pontifical Academy of Sciences, Pope John Paul II said:

> It is by virtue of his spiritual soul that the whole person possesses such a dignity even in his body. Pius XII stressed this essential point: If the human body takes its origin from pre-existent living matter, the spiritual soul is immediately created by God. . . .
>
> Consequently, theories of evolution which . . . consider the spirit as emerging from the forces of living matter . . . are incompatible with the truth about man. Nor are they able to ground the dignity of the person.[16]

Since it is impossible for our spiritual souls to have evolved, we can rest easy. Our remote ancestors definitely were not chimpanzees swinging from the family tree. We can count on the divinely created "dignity of the human race and the oneness of its origin and destiny."[17] As Pope Benedict XVI put it in his homily at the Mass for the inauguration of his pontificate, "We are not some casual and meaningless product of evolution. Each of us is the result of a thought of God. Each of us is willed, each of us is loved, each of us is necessary."[18]

Endnotes

1   *Genesis* 1–31; 2:1–2.

2   *CCC*, no. 329.

3   Trese, *The Faith Explained*, 29.

4   *Ibid.*, 30.

5   *CCC*, no. 332.

6   *CCC*, no. 334, citing *Acts* 5:18–20; 8:26–29; 10:3–8; 12:6–11; 27:23–25.

7   *CCC*, no. 336, quoting Saint Basil, *Adv. Eunomium* III, 1.

8   *Genesis* 1:27.

9   *CCC*, no. 355.

10 *CCC*, no. 356, quoting *Gaudium et Spes*, nos. 12 and 24.

11 *CCC*, no. 375, quoting Council of Trent (1546) and *Lumen Gentium*, no. 2.

12 *CCC*, nos. 376, 378, citing *Genesis* 2:17; 3:16, 19; 2:25; 2:8; 2:15; and 3:17–19.

13 Pope Pius XII, *Humani Generis* (1950), no. 37.

14 Cardinal Joseph Ratzinger, Address to Consistory of the College of Cardinals, Apr. 4, 1991, "The Problem of Threats to Human Life," *L'Osservatore Romano*, English ed. (Apr. 8, 1991): 2; 36 *The Pope Speaks*: 332 (1991). *Genesis* 3:20.

15 *CCC*, no. 366, citing Pius XII, *Humani Generis* (1950); Paul VI, *Credo* of the People of God (1968); Lateran Council V (1513).

16 26 *Origins* (Dec. 5, 1996): 414, 415.

17 Cardinal Joseph Ratzinger, "The Problem of Threats to Human Life," *L'Osservatore Romano*, English ed. (April 8, 1991): 2; 36 *The Pope Speaks*: 332, 333 (1991).

18 http://www.vatican.va/holy_Father/Benedict_xvi/homilies/ 2005/documents/hf_Ben-xvi_hom_20050424_inizio_pontific"to_ en.html.

9. SO GOD MADE *ME* IN HIS IMAGE?!
HOW? AND WHAT DIFFERENCE
DOES IT MAKE?

Why should I think that a low-voltage specimen like me is made in the image and likeness of the One who is all-perfect, all-knowing, etc.? The answer: I have to take the word of *Genesis* for it:

> Then God said, "Let us make man in our image, after our likeness. Let them have dominion over the fish of the sea, the birds of the air, and the cattle, and over all the wild animals and all the creatures that crawl on the ground." God created man in his image; / in the divine image he created him; / male and female he created them.[1]

Wait a minute. I have a body. God is a spirit. How can I be in his image?

The *Catechism* spells it out. Briefly, we are in the image and likeness of God because, like God, we have intellect and will. "By virtue of his soul and his spiritual powers of intellect and will, man is endowed with freedom, an 'outstanding manifestation of the divine image.'"[2] As we saw in Chapter 8, the only other creatures with intellect and will are the angels, who are pure spirits, persons without bodies. Because they were created with intellect and will, the angels were able to choose whether or not to love God and be with him forever, in eternal happiness, in heaven. Man is the only other creature who was created with intellect and will:

> Of all visible creatures only man is "able to know and love his Creator." . . . [H]e alone is called to share, by knowledge and love, in God's own life. It was for this end that he was created, and this is the fundamental reason for his dignity.[3]

Because he was created with intellect and free will, "the human individual possesses the dignity of a person, who is not just something, but someone. He is capable of self-knowledge, of self-possession and of freely giving himself and entering into communion with other persons. And he is called by grace to a covenant with his Creator, to offer him a response of faith and love that no other creature can give in his stead."[4]

Man, as a person, is superior to material creation. Therefore, he is "the only creature on earth that God has willed for its own sake."[5] The plants and animals are subjected to the use of man:

> God created everything for man, but man in turn was created to serve and love God and to offer all creation back to him:

> > "What is it that is about to be created, that enjoys such honor? It is man – that great and wonderful living creature, more precious in the eyes of God than all other creatures! For him the heavens and the earth, the sea and all the rest of creation exist. God attached so much importance to his salvation that he did not spare his own Son for the sake of man. Nor does he ever cease to work, trying every possible means, until he has raised man up to himself and made him sit at his right hand."[6]

So how does my body figure into this?

Relax: We are unities of body and soul. Here, again, the *Catechism* straightens it out:

> "The human person, created in the image of God, is a being at once corporeal and spiritual. . . . Man, whole and entire, is . . . *willed* by God."[7]

The human body shares in the dignity of "the image of God": it is a human body precisely because it is animated by a spiritual soul, and it is the whole human person that is intended to become, in the body of Christ, a temple of the Spirit:

> "Man, though made of body and soul, is a unity. . . . [M]an may not despise his bodily life. Rather he is obliged to regard his body as good and to hold it in honor since God has created it and will raise it up on the last day."[8]

The Church teaches that every spiritual soul is created immediately by God – it is not "produced" by the parents – and also that it is immortal: it does not perish when it separates from the body at death, and it will be reunited with the body at the final Resurrection.[9]

Chapters 16 and 17 will explore other aspects of our creation in the image and likeness of God, including our relation to others and how we can fulfill ourselves as persons by making a gift of self to God and our neighbor. But for now, note that God created each of us with intellect and will and the gift of freedom, so that we can seek God, freely choose to love Him, and someday obtain eternal happiness. Or we can choose to reject him.

The image of God in which man was created was obscured by original sin, which left us with an inclination to evil that can cause us to reject God by choosing evil. But God did not leave us without direction. In his love for us, he built into our nature a desire to know the truth and to seek the good. This desire orients us toward him, just as a compass always points north. He also

gave us the Commandments, which are specifications of that natural law, so that we will know what to do to achieve our ultimate objective of happiness in heaven. And God gently reminds us of our objective when we stray. Isn't it true that even when we seem to have everything we need to make us happy, we still feel there's something lacking?

Saint Augustine (354– 430) seemed to have it all in worldly terms. He was a brilliant young man who was successful professionally. He had a mistress and a close circle of friends, and he had embraced Manicheanism, a permissive pagan religion that provided him with a justification for his decadent lifestyle. His mother, Saint Monica, prayed incessantly for his conversion. As far as conversion was concerned, he seemed to be a hopeless case. Yet even then, he himself was conscious of something missing. He only experienced peace after his conversion to Christianity. Reflecting on this, Saint Augustine wrote:

> Man is one of your creatures, Lord, and his instinct is to praise you. He bears about him the mark of death, the sign of his own sin, to remind him that you thwart the

proud. But still, since he is a part of your creation, he wishes to praise you. The thought of you stirs him so deeply that he cannot be content unless he praises you, because you made us for yourself and our hearts find no peace until they rest in you.[10]

With his conversion, as Augustine later wrote, "a light as it were of serenity infused into my heart, all the darkness of doubt vanished away."[11] He had returned to the image and likeness of God in which he had been created and which he had obscured by his sins.

That creation gives each human person his dignity. The term "dignity" is often cheapened today; "death with dignity" is used as a code word for euthanasia. The real dignity of the human person arises from the fact that he is a child of God, created for a destiny of happiness forever in heaven. Cardinal Joseph Ratzinger, before he became Pope Benedict XVI, made this point in his 1991 address to the College of Cardinals:

> To sum up everything, then, we can say that the ultimate root of hatred for human life, of all attacks on human life, is the loss of God. Where God disappears, the absolute dignity of human life disappears as well. In light of the revelation concerning the creation of man in the image and likeness of God, the intangible sacredness of the human person has appeared. Only this divine dimension guarantees the full dignity of the human person. . . . In the struggle for life, talking about God is indispensable. . . . [O]nly in this way does the value of the weak, of the disabled, of the nonproductive, of the incurably ill become apparent; only in this way can we relearn and rediscover, too, the value of suffering: the greatest lesson on human dignity always remains the cross of Christ; our salvation has its origin not in what the Son of God did, but in his suffering, and whoever does not know how to suffer does not know how to live.[12]

The reality that we have dignity because of our creation should affect how we treat others and how we allow others to treat us. God calls us to treat everyone, no matter how poor or helpless, as a child of God with an intrinsic worth and dignity. It might not be a bad idea to think about that.

Called to be unconditionally pro-life

As we will see in Chapters 21, 22, and 23, the philosophers of what Pope John Paul II called "the culture of death" teach that all rights are conferred by the state, including the right to life. Only those with sufficient ability and usefulness are judged to be worthy of having rights. John Paul described this as "*a war of the powerful against the weak*: A life which would require greater acceptance, love and care is considered useless, or held to be an intolerable burden, and is therefore rejected in one way or another. A person who, because of illness, handicap or, more simply, just by existing, compromises the well-being or life-style of those who are more favoured tends to be looked upon as an enemy to be resisted or eliminated. In this way a kind of *conspiracy against life* is unleashed."[13]

Once that sort of "conspiracy against life" goes into motion, it gains momentum. In the Knauer case, in late 1938, Adolf Hitler authorized euthanasia, at the request of the grandmother or the father (the record is unclear) of a blind "idiot" infant born with one leg and part of one arm missing. Knauer was the "test case" that "was pivotal for the two killing programs of children and of adults."[14] Within months, as noted below in Chapter 24, the grounds for killing included such defects as cleft palates and "badly modeled ears." Those programs evolved into the Holocaust.[15]

In 1973, the United States Supreme Court ruled that the unborn child is not a "person" and is therefore not entitled to the right to life protected by the Constitution.[16] Over 40 million unborn children have been legally executed since that decision. But if we can declare the unborn child to be a nonperson with no right to live, we can do the same thing, in effect, to his older brother or his grandmother. Once we lose sight of the nature of man as an immortal child of God created in God's own image, the movement of the law becomes a utilitarian race to the bottom. Chapters 23 and 24 cover the accelerating rejection of human dignity in the developing law on abortion and euthanasia. For now we merely note that the creation of each human person in the image and likeness of God provides the only coherent basis for an absolute right of innocent human life. Only in the teachings of the Catholic Church will we find an uncompromising affirmation of that reality.

Those teachings are not for Catholics only. No one wants to be treated in a demeaning and insulting way. Everyone is instinctively drawn to those who treat every person as an image of God. Blessed Teresa of Calcutta, a simple nun working in the slums of Calcutta, touched the whole world by her compassionate treatment of the poor and suffering. Pope John Paul II became a hero to generations of young people for his tireless proclamation of the dignity of the person. At the death of the Holy Father, millions of people, especially the young, flocked to Rome to attend his funeral. It was an impromptu World Youth Day. Millions more watched as the funeral service was shown around the world. Remarkably, many of those mourning his death were not Catholic, but all were drawn to him by a sense that he truly cared for all human beings.

Jesus offers me the truth about myself

The ultimate example for us, however, is Jesus Christ, true God and true man. We learn about the dignity of the person as we contemplate Christ, who "fully reveals man to himself and brings to light his most high calling."[17] "God," said John Paul II, "has imprinted his own image and likeness on man . . . , conferring upon him an incomparable dignity. . . . From the Christian vision of the human person there necessarily follows a correct picture of society."[18]

Christ not only gave us his example, he remains with us in the Eucharist as a powerhouse from which (or, more precisely, from *whom*) we can draw the grace to grow in the love of God and love for others who also are made in his image and likeness. Blessed Teresa of Calcutta shows how the love of Jesus in the Eucharist helps us to love others. "After a short course with the medical mission sisters in Patna, Mother Teresa returned to Calcutta and found temporary lodging with the Little Sisters of the Poor. On 21 December she went for the first time to the slums. She visited families, washed the sores of some children, cared for an old man lying sick on the road and nursed a woman dying of hunger and TB. She started each day in communion with Jesus in the Eucharist and then went out, rosary in her hand, to find and serve him in *'the unwanted, the unloved, the uncared for.'*"[19]

Does Blessed Teresa of Calcutta strike us as an extreme example? If so, consider this. What would we do if we saw Jesus lying sick on the road? More important, what would Jesus do if he saw us unwanted, unloved, and uncared for? We are each an image of God – it's up to us to show it!

Endnotes

1 *Genesis* 1:26–27, New American Bible translation.

2 *CCC*, no. 1705, quoting *Gaudium et Spes*, no. 17.

3 *CCC*, no. 356, quoting *Gaudium et Spes*, no. 12.

4 *CCC*, no. 357.

5 *CCC*, no. 356, quoting *Gaudium et Spes*, no. 24.

6 *CCC*, no. 358, citing *Gaudium et Spes*, nos. 12, 24, 39, and quoting Saint John Chrysostom, *In Gen. Sermo II.*

7 *CCC*, no. 362, citing *Genesis* 2:7.

8 *CCC*, no. 364, citing *1 Corinthians* 6:19–20; 15:44–45; and *Dan* 3:57–80; quoting *Gaudium et Spes*, no. 14.

9 *CCC*, no. 366, citing Pius XII, *Humani Generis* (1950); Paul VI, *Credo* of the People of God (1968); and Lateran Council V (1513).

10 Saint Augustine, *Confessions*, Book I, no. 1 (Penguin Classics ed. 1961), p. 21.

11 Saint Augustine, *Confessions* Book VIII, no. 29 (Chicago: University of Chicago Press, 1952), 61.

12 Cardinal Joseph Ratzinger, "The Problem of Threats to Human Life," *L'Osservatore Romano*, English ed. (Apr. 8, 1991), p. 2; 36 *The Pope Speaks* 332, 343 (1991).

13 *EV,* no. 12.

14 Robert Jay Lifton, *The Nazi Doctors* (New York: Basic Books, 1986), 51.

15 *Ibid.*, Chapter 6.

16 *Roe v. Wade*, 410 U.S. 113 (1973).

17 Vatican II, *Gaudium et Spes* (*Pastoral Constitution on the Church in the Modern World*), no. 22; see *VS*, no. 2.

18 *CA*, nos. 11 and 13. On the human community in general, see *CCC*, nos. 1877–1948.

19 Biography of Blessed Teresa of Calcutta in Canonization proceedings (October 19, 2003). http://www.vatican.va/news_services/liturgy/Saints/ns_lit_doc_ 20031019_madre-teresa_en.html/.

10. HOW DID IT ALL GO WRONG?

God created man for the same reason he created the angels: in his goodness and love he intended man to share in the life of the Trinity, in perfect happiness, for all eternity.

Adam and Eve had it made

God created Adam and Eve with three levels of gifts. The first was the *natural*, their ordinary human nature in all its aspects: body and soul, including the intellect and will, which are faculties of the soul. The second was the *preternatural*. The preternatural gifts were extraordinary natural gifts, unusual natural perfections not ordinarily found in human nature. These included infused knowledge (Adam and Eve did not have to study); freedom from disease, suffering and death; and the gift of integrity, which means that they were not subject to any conflict between their natural urges and their reason; Adam and Eve had extraordinary will power and control of their passions and senses.

In addition to the natural and preternatural gifts, God gave a third and most important gift to Adam and Eve – the *supernatural*. The prefix, *super*, means above. This supernatural gift was the power to rise above their nature to share in the life of the Trinity. If the author of this chapter were able to give her dog, Casey, the power to share in the social life of her family, to say at the dinner table, "Please pass the salt," to offer suggestions for the family vacation, etc., to watch television and to ask, "What's on ESPN?", she would be giving Casey a supernatural gift. It is above the nature of a dog to sit down and discuss politics or to say, "Let's watch Monday night football." If she gave Casey the power to participate in the social life of the family, she would be raising her above her nature. Of her own power, Casey is absolutely incapable of raising herself to human level. So it is with God and man. There is no way that man, a created being, could raise himself, by his own power, to the level of participation in the social life of the Creator, God, the Holy Trinity. Yet God, in creating man, gave him this supernatural gift. At the end of their lives on earth, Adam and Eve would not have died. Instead, God would have taken them to Heaven to share in the life of God himself in total and unending happiness. This gift is above human nature. It is a supernatural gift.

As with the angels, all Adam and Eve had to do to win eternal happiness was to choose to love God, which includes the choice to acknowledge and obey him as Creator and Lord. "It is of the very nature of genuine love to make a complete surrender of self to the one who is loved. In this life, there is only one way in which love for God can prove itself – by the doing of God's will, by obedience to Him."[1] God gave to Adam and Eve a commandment: "And the Lord God commanded the Man thus: ''From every tree of the garden you may eat; but from the tree of the knowledge of good and evil you must not eat; for the day you eat of it, you must die."[2] "The symbol is clear: man was in no position to . . . decide for himself what was good and what was evil, but was constrained to appeal to a higher source."[3]

They blew it

"[T]here had to be a commandment so that there could be an act of obedience; there had to be an act of obedience so there could be a proof of love, a free and deliberate choosing of God in preference to self."[4] Adam and Eve disobeyed this commandment. "We do not know the exact nature of the first human sin. Scripture suggests that the malice of that sin lay chiefly in its elements of pride and disobedience."[5] The important question is not whether there really was an apple that they ate. Rather, the essential thing is that these real people, Adam and Eve, deliberately chose to disobey God. In their pride, they believed the serpent when he said to Eve that if she ate the fruit she would be "like God,"[6] no longer "dependent on [their] Creator," and no longer "subject to the laws of creation and to the moral norms that govern the use of freedom."[7] "[P]ride deceived our first parents into thinking themselves sovereign . . . and into thinking that they could ignore the knowledge which comes from God."[8] They thought that they themselves, "like God," would decide what was right and what was wrong. This is what we call Original Sin, the first sin of the human race.

The *Catechism of the Catholic Church* explains the consequences of Original Sin:

> God created man in his image and established him in his friendship. A spiritual creature, man can live this friendship only in free submission to God. . . . The "tree of the knowledge of good and evil" symbolically evokes the insurmountable limits that man, being a creature, must freely recognize and respect with trust. Man is dependent on his Creator and subject to the laws of creation and to the moral norms that govern the use of freedom.

> Man, . . . disobeyed God's command. This is . . . man's first sin. . . . All subsequent sin would be disobedience toward God and lack of trust in his goodness.

> The harmony in which they had found themselves . . . is now destroyed: the control of the soul's spiritual faculties over the body is shattered; the union of man and woman becomes subject to tensions, their relations henceforth marked by lust and domination. . . . [V]isible creation has become alien and hostile to man. . . . Finally, the consequence . . . foretold for this disobedience will come

true: man will "return to the ground" . . . *Death makes
its entrance into human history.*

After that first sin, the world is virtually inundated by
sin. There is Cain's murder of his brother Abel and the
universal corruption which follows in the wake of sin.
. . . And even after Christ's atonement, sin raises its head
in countless ways among Christians. Scripture and the
Church's Tradition continually recall the presence and
universality of sin in man's history.[9]

And they blew it for me

"By his sin Adam, as the first man, lost the original holiness
and justice he had received from God, not only for himself but
for all human beings."[10] Had Adam and Eve been faithful we
would have inherited all their gifts. But when they sinned, they
lost their preternatural and supernatural gifts and had nothing
left to hand down to us except their natural gifts. We are subject
to suffering, and we will die. Instead of the integrity and self-
control that Adam and Eve were given, we have an inclination to
evil. This disordered inclination is called Concupiscence, "the
movement of the sensitive appetite contrary to the operation of
the human reason. The apostle St. Paul identifies it with the
rebellion of the 'flesh' against the 'spirit.'"[11] Most important, we
come into this life without the supernatural gift of sanctifying
grace, with no right to heaven and no way to get there. The next
chapter will tell me how Christ has restored to us this opportunity to gain eternal happiness.

Is it unjust that we come into the world without the preternatural and supernatural gifts lost by Adam and Eve? No. Justice
requires that a person receive that to which he is entitled. We had
no right to be created with those gifts. As creatures, we had no
claim on God to heaven, to participate eternally in the life of the
Trinity; we had no right to the preternatural gifts, nor even to be
created at all.

Suppose your grandfather were told by his own father that he would give him $5 million if he abstained from alcoholic beverages until his 21st birthday. If your grandfather successfully abstained from drinking and received that money, you as his descendant would be a very wealthy person in terms of today's

inflated currency. If, however, your grandfather took a drink the night before his 21st birthday, he would not have received the money. You would not now have the wealth you would have inherited had he lived up to the bargain. However, your great-grandfather, in withholding the money from his son, your grandfather, did no injustice. Your grandfather had no right to that money since he did not keep his end of the bargain. Your great-grandfather did not treat you unjustly in refusing to pay to his son the money which the son failed to earn. You have no right to that money. So it is with original sin, the failure of your first parents, Adam and Eve, to live up to their bargain with God. It is not unjust when, as a result of the sin of Adam and Eve, we come into the world without the preternatural and supernatural gifts to which we have no right. We have no right to those gifts; indeed, we have no right to be created at all.

Actual sin, whether mortal or venial, is the sin we ourselves commit. But all human persons since Adam and Eve, except for the Blessed Virgin Mary, are conceived with original sin. "By yielding to the tempter, Adam and Eve committed a *personal sin*, but this sin affected the *human nature* that they would then transmit *in a fallen state*."[12] "The story of original sin and its part in the life of every human being . . . offers the key to . . . many problems facing us in the twentieth century as well as at the dawn of civilization. Why sickness and suffering? Why cannot we just let children 'express themselves' and grow up 'naturally'? Why do we have to fight against sin and temptation instead of 'coasting along' through life? The answer to all those questions will not be difficult to fathom if we realize the teaching of the Catholic Church on original sin."[13]

Endnotes

1 Trese, *The Faith Explained*, 53.

2 *Genesis* 2:15–17.

3 *FR*, no. 22.

4 Trese, The Faith Explained, 45.

5 Ronald Lawler, O.F.M. Cap., Donald W. Wuerl and Thomas C. Lawler, *The Teaching of Christ* (Huntington, Ind.: Our Sunday Visitor, 1975), 84.

6 *Genesis* 3:5.

7 *CCC*, no. 396.

8 *FR*, no. 22.

9 *CCC*, nos. 396, 397, 400, 401, quoting *Genesis* 2:17; 3:19; citing *Genesis* 2:17; 3:1–11; 3:7–16; 3:17, 19; *Romans* 5:12, 19, 21.

10 *CCC*, no. 416.

11 *CCC*, no. 2515, citing *Galatians* 5:16, 17, 24; *Ephesians* 2:3.

12 *CCC*, no. 404, citing Council of Trent (1546).

13 Edward J. Hayes, Paul J. Hayes, and James J. Drummey, *Catholicism and Reason* (Huntington, Ind.: Our Sunday Visitor, 1990), 186.

11. HOW – AND WHY – DID CHRIST FIX THE PROBLEM?

A second chance

God could have left mankind in its fallen state, with no chance of ever reaching heaven. But in his infinite, unlimited mercy and love, God promised that he would give man a second chance. However, since God is also infinitely just, reparation had to be made for the sin of man.

This is a familiar concept. If my neighbor smashed my living room window with a baseball, I would not be satisfied with a mere apology. Rather, my neighbor would be obliged in justice to make up for my loss, to repair the damage. This is reparation or atonement.

God's immediate response to the sin of Adam and Eve included a promise: A Redeemer who would set things right.[1] "This passage in Genesis is called the *Protoevangelium* ('first gospel'): the first announcement of the Messiah and Redeemer. . . . the 'New Adam' who, because he 'became obedient unto death, even death on a cross,' makes amends superabundantly for the disobedience of Adam."[2]

Why did it have to be Jesus Christ?

Reparation for the sin of man should be made by man. But the gravity of an offense is measured by the dignity of the person offended. When Pope John Paul II was shot in 1981, it shocked the world; it was because the gravity of the offense was increased by the dignity and stature of the victim. But sin is an offense against God. Since God is of infinite dignity, the offense against God, committed by man, was infinite. Infinite means unlimited. No individual man or number of men could make up for that sin because man is not infinite. A reparation of infinite value is required for an infinite offense. But who could make infinite reparation to God but God himself? To fulfill his promise that he would give man a second chance, God himself, the Second Person of the Trinity, took on human nature so that he, as man, could make reparation for the sin of man and so that, as God, his reparation would be an infinite satisfaction for the infinite offense against God. The Second Person of the Trinity had no beginning because he is God from all eternity. But when the Angel Gabriel, at the Annunciation,[3] informed the Blessed Mother that she was to be the mother of God, and she accepted, God the Son became man. This is the Incarnation, meaning that God the Son took on human nature. "Incarnation" comes from the Latin word, *caro*, meaning flesh. As John's Gospel puts it, "And the Word was made flesh, and dwelt among us."[4]

God the Son, Jesus Christ, became man to redeem us. If I pawn a watch, I can get it back if I redeem it by paying back what I borrowed on it, with interest. As God and man, Christ redeemed each of us. He paid the price to satisfy the infinite justice of God. He restored to us the gift of eternal life. We can accept this gift by loving and obeying God, or we can reject it by sin.

Who and what is Jesus Christ?

"We . . . confess . . . one God in three persons. . . . The divine persons do not share the one divinity among themselves but each of them is God whole and entire."[5] Christ is one person of the Trinity. He is a divine person. As such he possessed from all eternity the divine nature possessed by all three persons in the Trinity. But, unlike the Father and the Holy Spirit, the Second

Person assumed a human nature as well. This union of a divine nature and a human nature in one divine person, Jesus Christ, is called the Hypostatic Union. The Council of Chalcedon, in 451, defined this doctrine:

> Following the holy Fathers, we unanimously teach and confess one and the same Son, our Lord Jesus Christ: the same perfect in divinity and perfect in humanity, the same truly God and truly man, composed of rational soul and body; consubstantial with the Father as to his divinity and consubstantial with us as to his humanity; "like us in all things but sin." He was begotten from the Father before all ages as to his divinity and in these last days, for us and for our salvation, was born as to his humanity of the virgin Mary, the Mother of God.
>
> We confess that one and the same Christ, Lord, and only-begotten Son, is to be acknowledged in two natures without confusion, change, division, or separation. The distinction between the natures was never abolished by their union, but rather the character proper to each of the two natures was preserved as they came together in one person *(prosopon)* and one hypostasis.[6]

Father John A. Hardon, S.J., summarized the "essentials" of this doctrine on the divine person, Christ:

What are these essentials?

✳ that Christ assumed a real and not just an apparent body. He was born of a woman, from whom he received a truly human nature.

✳ that in becoming man, he assumed not only a body but also a rational soul, with intellect and will. Christ therefore had a divine and human mind, a divine and human will.

✳ that the two natures in Christ are united to form one individual. Christ is one person, the second person of the Trinity.

✳ that in Christ each of the two natures remains unimpaired, they are not confused or changed in their respective properties; nor are they divided or separated, as though merely co-existing side by side.

✳ that in becoming man, Christ was and remains true God, one in nature with the Father. When Saint Paul speaks of God "emptying himself" to become man, this does not mean that God somehow ceased to be God.

✳ that even as man, Christ is absolutely sinless. He not only did not sin, but he could not sin because he was God. Only in the spurious supposition that Christ has two persons is sin conceivable, since the human person might then commit sin, while the divine person would be perfectly holy. Since Christ was utterly sinless, he was also free from concupiscence or unruly passions, and also free from such effects of concupiscence as positive ignorance or error.

✳ that the reason for the Incarnation was redemptive. Christ was born into the world "for our salvation," to undergo the meritorious death that, except for this mortality, would have been impossible.

✳ that Mary is consequently not only Mother of Christ but Mother of God, since he was "born of Mary" in time who is begotten of the Father in eternity.

✳ that, since the Savior was one person, whatever he did (or does) was (and is) done simultaneously by both natures, although in different ways. When Christ talked and walked and ate and slept and died, it was the God-man who did all these things. When he worked the miracles of healing disease, calming the storm at sea, and raising the dead, it too was the God-man who did all these things. Now at the right hand of his Father, it is the same God-man who is our heavenly high priest and who on the last day will come to judge the living and the dead.[7]

What was he really like?

"During the greater part of his life Jesus shared the condition of the vast majority of human beings: a daily life spent without evident greatness, a life of manual labor. His religious life was that of a Jew obedient to the law of God, a life in the community."[8] Jesus Christ is truly both God and man. "To the question 'Who are you?' Christ would have but one answer. He is the Second Person of the Blessed Trinity, God the Son, the Word. But to the question 'What are you?' Christ our Lord would have two answers, for He has two natures; He is God and He is man."[9] Saint Luke tells us that, after Mary and Joseph found him teaching in the temple, he went home with them and was obedient to them.[10] "And Jesus advanced in wisdom and age and grace before God and men."[11]

Did Christ have to learn things? Did he make mistakes? Did he know who he was? "[B]ecause Jesus had two natures, the human and divine, he also had two kinds of knowledge. He had the infinite knowledge which God has: the knowledge of all things. Jesus had this knowledge, of course, from the very beginning of His existence in Mary's womb."[12] Pope Saint Pius X, in 1907, formally condemned the proposition that "Christ did not always have the consciousness of his messianic dignity."[13] Christ knew he was God and never had an identity crisis.

As a human being, Jesus had another kind of knowledge, his human knowledge. His human knowledge, in turn, was of three kinds. First there was the *beatific knowledge* which his human nature had from the moment of his conception, a knowledge which was the result of his human nature being united to a divine nature. This is similar to the knowledge which you and I will have when we see God in heaven. But there also was in Jesus an *infused knowledge*, such as God gave to the angels and to Adam. It is a knowledge directly conferred by God, a complete knowledge of created things, a knowledge that does not have to be laboriously reasoned out from the evidences supplied by the senses. There also was in Jesus the *experimental knowledge*, the knowledge-by-experience, which he acquired as He grew and developed. . . . Jesus knew from the beginning what it would be like, for example, to walk. But he acquired the experimental knowledge of what it is like to walk only when His legs were strong enough to bear Him.[14]

The *Catechism* offers a helpful explanation of the interaction of the human and divine knowledge of Christ:

This human soul that the Son of God assumed is endowed with a true human knowledge. As such, this knowledge could not in itself be unlimited: it was exercised in the historical conditions of his existence in space and time. This is why the Son of God could, when he became man, "increase in wisdom and in stature, and in favor with God and man," and would even have to inquire for himself about what one in the human condition can learn only from experience. This corresponded to the reality of his voluntary emptying of himself, taking "the form of a slave." . . .

But at the same time, this truly human knowledge of God's Son expressed the divine life of his person. "The human nature of God's son, *not by itself but by its union with the Word*, knew and showed forth in itself everything that pertains to God." Such is first of all the case with the intimate and immediate knowledge that the Son of God made man has of his Father. The Son in his human knowledge also showed the divine penetration he had into the secret thoughts of human hearts.

By its union to the divine wisdom in the person of the

Word incarnate, Christ enjoyed in his human knowledge the fullness of understanding of the eternal plans he had come to reveal. What he admitted to not knowing in this area, he elsewhere declared himself not sent to reveal. [cf. Mark 13:32; Acts 1:7][15]

Christ is one divine person. He "could operate, really and truly, in both natures. If Our Lord wanted to lift a load, He could have lifted it either by the effortless fiat of the divine will or by the hard effort of the human muscles."[16] But he chose to gain human knowledge experimentally. Christ had two intellects and two wills, divine and human. His human intellect and will were subject to his divine intellect and will. "[T]he Word made flesh willed humanly in obedience to his Father all that he had decided divinely with the Father and the Holy Spirit for our salvation."[17] He chose to learn how to drive a nail as any other boy would learn it; like any other boy learning the trade he probably hit his thumb on occasion. But he always possessed the divine power.

Every act of a divine person is of infinite value. It was not necessary for Christ to undergo what he went through in order to redeem us. The smallest act on his part would have been infinitely valuable and sufficient. "Jesus' violent death was not the result of chance in an unfortunate coincidence of circumstances, but is part of the mystery of God's plan."[18] The fact that Christ chose to suffer and to die for us on Calvary is a measure of his love for me. As Saint Alphonsus Liguori, a Doctor of the Church, put it:

> Jesus Christ could easily have obtained for us salvation without suffering. Would it not have sufficed for him to have offered to his eternal Father one single prayer for the pardon of man? For this prayer, being of infinite value, would have been sufficient to save the world, and infinite worlds besides. Why, then, did he choose for himself so much suffering, and a death so cruel. . . ? To

what purpose so much cost in order to save man? . . .
Because Jesus loved us so much, he desired to be loved
very much by us; and therefore he did everything that he
could, even unto suffering for us, in order to conciliate
our love, and to show that there was nothing more that
he could do to make us love him.[19]

The "Paschal Mystery," in the words of Benedict XVI,
"refers to Christ's Passion, his Death and Resurrection, and his
Ascension."[20] "The Paschal mystery of Christ's cross and
Resurrection stands at the center of the Good News that the
apostles, and the Church . . . are to proclaim to the world."[21] The
word, "Paschal," refers either to the Jewish feast of the Passover
or to Easter since Christ died and rose at the time of Passover.
The term, "Paschal mystery," as we use it, "has two aspects: by
his death, Christ liberates us from sin; by his Resurrection, he
opens for us the way to a new life."[22] The Resurrection of Jesus
"was an historical event that could be verified by the sign of the
empty tomb and by the reality of the apostles' encounters with
the risen Christ."[23] Yet it is also "something that transcends and
surpasses history. . . . a transcendent intervention of God himself
in creation and history."[24] His resurrection confirms Christ's
divinity and his teachings.[25] And it is a promise of our own resurrection at the end of time.[26]

The life of Jesus Christ, including especially his passion and
death, is a love story.

Endnotes

1 *Genesis* 3:9, 15.

2 *CCC*, nos. 410, 411, citing *1 Corinthians* 15:21–22, 45; *Philemon*
   2:8; *Romans* 5:19–20.

3 *Luke* 1:26–38.

4 *John* 1:14.

5 *CCC*, no. 253, citing Council of Constantinople II (553).

6 *CCC*, no. 467, quoting Council of Chalcedon (451), citing
   Hebrews 4:15.

7   John A. Hardon, S.J., *The Catholic Catechism* (Doubleday, 1975), 140–41.

8   *CCC*, no. 531, citing *Galatians* 4:4.

9   Frank Sheed, *Theology and Sanity* (Our Sunday Visitor, 1978), 162.

10 *Luke* 2:51; *CCC*, no. 531.

11 *Luke*, 2:52.

12 Leo J. Trese, *The Faith Explained* (Sinag-tala, Manila, 1991), 67.

13 Pope Saint Pius X, *Decree Lamentabili Sane* (1907).

14 Trese, *The Faith Explained*, 67–68 (Emphasis added).

15 *CCC*, nos. 472, 473, 474, quoting *Lk* 2:52; *Philemon* 2:7; Saint Maximus the Confessor, *Qu. et dub.* 66; citing Saint Gregory the Great, *"Sicut aqua" ad Eulogium, Epist. Lib* 10; *Matthew* 11:27; *Mark* 2:8; 6:38; 8:27, 31; 9:31; 10:33–34; 13:32; 14:18–20, 26–30, 36; *John* 1:18; 2:25; 6:61; 8:55; 11:34; *Acts* 1:7.

16 Frank Sheed, *Theology and Sanity* (Our Sunday Visitor, 1978), 166.

17 *CCC*, no. 475, citing Council of Constantinople III.

18 *CCC*, no. 599.

19 Saint Alphonsus Liguori, *The Passion and the Death of Jesus Christ* (Brooklyn, N.Y.: Redemptorist Fathers, 1927), 33–34.

20 Pope Benedict XVI, Address to Youth, April 19, 2008.

21 *CCC*, no. 571.

22 *CCC*, no. 654.

23 *CCC*, no. 647.

24 *CCC*, nos. 647, 648.

25 *CCC*, nos. 651, 653.

26 See *1 Corinthians* 15.

12. HOW IS CHRIST WITH ME TODAY?

Christ came on earth to redeem me. To carry on his work after his ascension into Heaven, he founded a Church.

Which Church is the one founded by Christ and how would I recognize it today? Any organization claiming to be the Church founded by Christ would have to possess four marks or characteristics. It must be *"one, holy, catholic, and apostolic."*[1]

1. The Church must be one.[2]

"The Church is one because of her source: . . . 'the unity, in the Trinity of Persons, of one God, the Father and the Son in the Holy Spirit.'"[3] "The Church is one *because of her founder*: for 'The Word made flesh, the prince of peace, reconciled all men to God by the cross, . . . restoring the unity of all in one people and one body.'"[4] "The Church is one *because of her 'soul'*: 'It is the Holy Spirit, dwelling in those who believe and . . . ruling over the entire Church, who . . . joins [the faithful] together so intimately in Christ.'"[5]

"The Church is the Body of Christ."[6] "What the soul is to the human body, the Holy Spirit is to . . . the Church."[7] Because of this Trinitarian unity, there can be only one Church founded by Christ. "From the beginning, this one Church has been marked by a great *diversity*. . . . Within the unity of the People of God, a multiplicity of peoples and cultures is gathered together."[8] But they must be united in one "faith received from the Apostles"; in "common celebration of divine worship"; and in "apostolic succession."[9] The words of our Lord reinforce the conclusion that

his Church must be one: "And other sheep I have that are not of this fold. Them also I must bring," Jesus says, "and they shall hear my voice, and there shall be one fold and one shepherd."[10] "This is why Jesus himself prayed at the hour of his Passion, and does not cease praying to his Father, for the unity of his disciples: 'That they may all be one. As you, Father, are in me and I am in you, may they also be one in us, . . . so that the world may know that you have sent me.' The desire to recover the unity of all Christians is a gift of Christ and a call of the Holy Spirit."[11] A supporting indication that Christ founded only one Church is the variety of contradictory answers to doctrinal and moral questions professed by communities that describe themselves as Christian. What is the Eucharist? Is it *really* the Body and Blood of Christ? Can a marriage be ended by divorce? Is abortion right or wrong? And so on. Contradictory answers cannot both be right. It is inconceivable that Jesus Christ, who "*is the Truth*"[12] would establish any church that would teach as true that which is false.

2. The Church must be holy.[13]

The Church is holy "because Christ . . . joined her to himself as his body and endowed her with the gift of the Holy Spirit for the glory of God."[14] Christ redeemed us to bring us closer to

God, that is, to make us holy. The Church founded by Christ must be one which of its nature tends to make people holy, to sanctify them. "United with Christ, the Church is sanctified by him; through him and with him she becomes sanctifying. 'All the activities of the Church are directed . . . to the sanctification of men in Christ and the glorification of God.' It is in the Church that 'the fullness of the means of salvation' has been deposited. It is in her that 'by the grace of God we acquire holiness.'"[15] To say that the Church is holy is not the same as saying that its members are all holy. The Church survives in spite of its members, not because of them. But the Church founded by Christ has to be holy in the sense described here.

3. The Church must be catholic.[16]

Catholic with a small 'c' means universal. "[T]he Church is catholic because she has been sent out by Christ on a mission to the whole of the human race."[17] The Church founded by Christ is for all men of all times, without distinction of race, sex, nationality, or otherwise. "And this gospel of the kingdom shall be preached in the whole world, for a witness to all nations."[18] "Go into the whole world and preach the gospel to every creature"[19] "[Y]ou shall be witnesses for me in Jerusalem and in all Judea and Samaria and even to the very ends of the earth."[20]

4. The Church must be apostolic.[21]

The Church founded by Christ must be able to trace its history and teaching in unbroken continuity to the Apostles. "And I say to thee, thou art Peter, and upon this rock I will build My Church, and the gates of hell shall not prevail against it."[22]

Only the Catholic Church can trace its lineage back to Peter, the first Pope appointed by Christ himself. The Lutheran church was founded by Martin Luther in 1524, the Episcopalian or Anglican church by Henry VIII in 1534, the Methodist Episcopal church by John Wesley in 1739, the Baptists by Roger Williams in 1639, the Quakers by George Fox in 1647, and so on.[23] "The Catholic Church," in the words of Cardinal

Gibbons, "can easily vindicate the title of Apostolic, because she derives her origin from the apostles. Every Priest and Bishop can trace his genealogy to the first disciples of Christ with as much facility as the most remote branch of a vine can be traced to the main stem. All the Catholic Clergy in the United States, for instance, were ordained only by Bishops who are in active communion with the See of Rome. These bishops themselves received their commissions from the Bishop of Rome. . . . Like the Evangelist Luke, who traces the genealogy of our Savior back to Adam and to God, we can trace the pedigree of Pius IX [or any Pope, including Benedict XVI] to Peter and to Christ. There is not a link wanting in the chain which binds the humblest Priest in the land to the Prince of the Apostles. . . . Count over the Bishops from the very See of St. Peter, and mark, in this list of Fathers, how one succeeded the other. This is the rock against which the proud gates of hell do not prevail."[24]

> The Catholic faithful *are required to profess* that there is an historical continuity – rooted in the apostolic succession – between the church founded by Christ and the Catholic Church: "This is the single church of Christ . . . which our Savior, after his resurrection, entrusted to Peter's pastoral care, commissioning him and the other Apostles to extend and rule her, erected for all ages as "the pillar and mainstay of the truth." This church, constituted and organized as a society in the present world, subsists in [*subsistit in*] the Catholic Church, governed by the successor of Peter and by the Bishops in communion with him." With the expression *subsistit in*, the Second Vatican Council sought to harmonize two doctrinal statements: on the one hand, that the church of Christ, despite the divisions which exist among Christians, continues to exist fully only in the Catholic Church, and on the other hand, that "outside her structure, many elements can be found of sanctification and truth," that is, in those churches and ecclesial communities which are not yet in full communion with the

Catholic Church. But with respect to these, it needs to be stated that "they derive their efficacy from the very fullness of grace and truth entrusted to the Catholic Church."[25]

In 2007, the Congregation for the Doctrine of the Faith, with the approval of Pope Benedict XVI, issued "Responses to Some Questions Regarding Certain Aspects of the Doctrine of the Church." The Congregation explained that "oriental Churches separated from full communion with the Catholic Church" can still be called "Churches" because they maintained the Eucharist and the succession of their bishops from the apostles. However, the "Christian Communities born out of the Reformation of the sixteenth century" are not "Churches." Rather, "[t]hese ecclesial communities which, specifically because of the absence of the sacramental priesthood, have not preserved the . . . substance of the Eucharistic Mystery cannot, according to Catholic doctrine, be called 'Churches' in the proper sense."[26]

The Catholic Church fully teaches the true religion. However, although "[t]he sole Church of Christ . . . subsists in the Catholic Church. . . . many elements of sanctification and of truth are found outside its visible confines."[27] Your Protestant friends, who have been baptized, are Christians. They have "elements of sanctification and truth," including "the written Word of God; the life of grace; faith, hope, and charity, with the other interior gifts of the Holy Spirit, as well as visible elements."[28] But they lack the fullness of the Faith which can be found only in the Catholic Church. "With non-Catholic Christians, Catholics must enter into a respectful dialogue of charity and truth, . . . in order that the fullness of the means of salvation can be offered to one's partners in dialogue. In this way, they are led to an ever deeper conversion to Christ."[29]

Only the Catholic Church

The Catholic Church, said the Second Vatican Council "is the unique Church of Christ which in the Creed we avow as one, holy, catholic, and apostolic."[30]

The Holy Spirit is "the principal agent of the whole of the

Church's mission." That mission of the Church "continues and, in the course of history, unfolds the mission of Christ."[31] In the performance of its mission, this Church founded by Christ has three functions:

* *To teach* on matters of faith and morals.

* *To rule*, that is, to establish disciplinary and regulatory standards for the governance of the Church.

* *To sanctify*, that is, to provide sanctifying and actual grace through the sacramental system and other means.[32]

The remaining chapters of this book discuss applications of the teaching function of the Church. We should note first, however, the importance of the sanctifying function, by which the Church helps us to draw close to God, that is, to be holy. The Church sanctifies especially through the liturgy and the sacraments. "Christ is always present in his Church, especially in her liturgical celebrations. He is present in the Sacrifice of the Mass . . . especially in the Eucharistic species."[33] The Holy Spirit, too, has a mission in the liturgy, "to prepare the assembly to encounter Christ; to recall and manifest Christ to the faith of the assembly; to make the saving work of Christ present and active by his transforming power; and to make the gift of communion bear fruit in the Church."[34] In his Church, "Christ now acts through the sacraments he instituted to communicate his grace."[35] The sacraments are "signs of grace, instituted by Christ and entrusted to the Church, by which divine life is dispensed to us."[36] Grace is "the *free and undeserved help* that God gives us to respond to his call."[37] There are several kinds of grace. Sanctifying grace, which we first receive in Baptism, is "the grace that justifies."[38] It is the "gift that God makes to us of his own life, infused by the Holy Spirit into our soul to heal it of sin and to sanctify it."[39] Actual graces are "God's interventions" to help us in specific circumstances.[40] Habitual grace is "the permanent disposition to live and act in keeping with God's call [as] distinguished from *actual graces* which [are] God's interventions."[41] And each sacrament brings its own "sacramental grace." For example, the sacrament of Penance or Reconciliation[42] confers "peace and serenity of conscience, and . . . spiritual strength."[43] Baptism, Confirmation and Holy Eucharist are called sacraments of Christian initiation because they "lay the *foundations* of every Christian life."[44] Penance and the Anointing of the Sick are called sacraments of healing.[45] Holy Orders and Matrimony are called sacraments at the service of communion and mission.[46]

The teaching, ruling and sanctifying functions of the Church work together to carry out the mission of the Church. That mission is "to proclaim and establish the Kingdom of God begun by Jesus Christ among all peoples."[47]

Endnotes

1   *CCC,* no. 865.

2   *CCC*, no. 813.

3   *CCC*, no. 813, quoting *Unitatis Redintegratio*, no. 2, §5.

4   *CCC*, no. 813, quoting *Gaudium et Spes*, no. 78, §3.

5   *CCC*, no. 813, quoting *Unitatis Redintegratio*, no. 2, §2.

6   *CCC*, no. 805.

7   *CCC*, no. 797, quoting St. Augustine, *Sermo* 267, 4.

8   *CCC*, no. 814.

9   *CCC*, no. 815.

10   *John* 10:16.

11   *CCC*, no. 820, quoting *John* 17:21 and citing *Hebrews* 7:25 and *Unitatis Redintegratio,* no. 1.

12   *CCC*, no. 2466, citing *John* 1:14, 8:12, and 14:6.

13   *CCC*, no. 823.

14   *CCC*, no. 823, quoting *Lumen Gentium*, no. 239, and citing *Eph.* 5:25–26.

15   *CCC*, no. 824, quoting *Sacrosanctum Concilium*, no. 10; *Unitatis Redintegratio*, no. 3; and *Lumen Gentium*, no. 48.

16   *CCC*, no. 830.

17   *CCC,* no. 831, citing *Matthew* 28:19.

18   *Matthew* 24:14.

19   *Mark* 16:15.

20   *Acts* 1:8.

21   *CCC*, no. 857.

22   *Matthew* 16:18.

23   See James Cardinal Gibbons, *The Faith of Our Fathers* (Notre Dame, Ind.: Cashel Institute, 1982), 34.

24   Ibid., 35–36.

25   Congregation for the Doctrine of the Faith, Declaration on the unicity and salvific universality of Jesus Christ and the Church, *Dominus Iesus* (August 6, 2000), no. 16 (citations omitted); *Dominus Iesus* was "ratified and confirmed" by Pope John Paul II, who "ordered its publication." *Dominus Iesus,* Conclusion.

26   See text of the document and discussion in Inside the Vatican, August/Sept. 2007, 11, 12.

27   *CCC*, no. 870, quoting *Lumen Gentium*, no. 8.

28   *CCC*, no. 819, quoting *Lumen Gentium*, no. 8, §2 and *Unitatis Redintegratio*, no. 3 §2 and citing *Lumen Gentium*, 15.

29   Congregation for the Doctrine of the Faith, Doctrinal Note on some Aspects of Evangelization (2007). See discussion in Inside the Vatican, August/Sept. 2007, 11, 12.

30   *Lumen Gentium*, no. 8.

31   *CCC*, no. 852, quoting John Paul II, *Redemptoris Missio*, no. 21, and *Ad Gentes*, no. 5.

32   See *CCC*, nos. 888–96.

33   *CCC*, no. 1088, quoting *Sacrosanctum Concilium*, no. 7.

34   *CCC*, no. 1112.

35   *CCC*, no. 1084.

36   *CCC*, no. 1131.

37   *CCC*, no. 1996.

38   *Compendium of the Catechism of the Catholic Church*, no. 423.

39   *CCC*, no. 1999.

40   *CCC*, no. 2000.

41   *CCC*, no. 2000.

42   *CCC*, nos. 1423–24.

43   *CCC*, no. 1496.

44   *CCC*, no. 1212.

45   *CCC*, no. 1420.

46   *CCC*, nos. 1533–35; *Compendium to CCC*, no. 250.

47   *Compendium to CCC*, no. 150.

13. THE CHURCH?! WHY DO I NEED IT?

Why should I listen to the Church?

Sometimes I may think of God as a kind of super-cop, setting arbitrary rules to keep me from having fun and being happy.

The reality is just the opposite, as described by the English Catholic author, Gilbert K. Chesterton:

> Catholic doctrine and discipline may be walls; but they are the walls of a playground. Christianity is the only frame which has preserved the pleasure of Paganism. We might fancy some children playing on the flat, grassy top of some tall island in the sea. So long as there was a wall round the cliff's edge they could fling themselves into every frantic game and make the place the noisiest of nurseries. But the walls were knocked down, leaving the naked peril of the precipice. The children did not fall over, but when their friends returned to them they were all huddled in terror in the center of the island; and their song had ceased.[1]

If my brand new Chevy had a flat tire on a country road late at night, what is the first thing I would do? I would look in the glove compartment and read the manual to find out where the jack is, how to use it, and how to change the tire. Would I resent the directions contained in that manual? Not likely. So why should I resent the teachings of the Church? They are like a manual provided, not by General Motors, but by God himself, my Creator, to show me how to achieve eternal happiness, a goal even more important than changing a tire.

"Go therefore," Christ told his apostles, "and make disciples of all nations, . . . teaching them to observe all that I have commanded you."[2] "Unless Christ's whole life – and death – were to be in vain, there had to be a living voice in the world which would proclaim Christ's teachings down through the centuries. . . . [I]t would have to be a visible speaker whom all men of good will could recognize as one having authority. Consequently, Jesus founded His Church not merely to sanctify mankind by means of the sacraments but first of all to *teach* mankind the truths which Jesus taught, the truths necessary for salvation. . . . [I]f Jesus had not founded a Church even the name of Jesus Christ would be unknown to us today."[3]

Can the Church ever be wrong?

The teaching Church consists of the Pope and the Bishops in union with the Pope.[4] The Church teaches on matters of faith and morals. It makes sense that the Church founded by Christ has the power to teach infallibly with immunity from even the possibility of error. "This . . . means . . . that the Church (either in the person of the Pope, or of all the Bishops together under the Pope) cannot make a mistake when she solemnly proclaims that a certain matter of belief or of conduct has been revealed by God and must be held and followed by all. Jesus Christ's promise, 'Behold, I am with you all days, even unto the consummation of the world' (Matthew 28:20) would be meaningless if his Church were not infallible. Certainly Jesus would not be with his Church if he allowed his Church to fall into error concerning the essentials of salvation. The Catholic knows that the Pope can sin, like any other human being. The Catholic knows that the Pope's personal opinions enjoy only as much standing as the Pope's human wisdom may give them, but the Catholic also knows that when the Pope, as the head of Christ's Church, publicly and solemnly proclaims that a certain truth has been revealed by Christ, either personally or through his apostles, Peter's successor cannot be in error. Jesus would not establish a Church which could lead men astray."[5]

The Church exercises infallibility not only in making a solemn proclamation but also in the exercise of the ordinary Magisterium or teaching authority of the Church. As the Second Vatican Council declared, the infallibility which Christ promised to his Church resides not only in the Pope when he is speaking *ex cathedra*, the Latin term meaning "from the chair" of Peter and with his full authority, but also "in the body of bishops when, together with Peter's successor, they exercise the supreme teaching office," either "in an ecumenical council" or "when, even though dispersed throughout the world but preserving . . . amongst themselves and with Peter's successor the bond of communion, in their authoritative teaching concerning matters of faith and morals, they are in agreement that a particular teaching is to be held definitively and absolutely."[6]

Note that every exercise of the power to teach infallibly requires the assent of the Pope. "The college or body of Bishops has . . . no authority unless united with the Roman Pontiff, Peter's successor, as its head . . . . For the Roman Pontiff, by reason of his office as Vicar of Christ . . . has full, supreme and universal power over the whole Church."[7] Christ gave the keys of the kingdom of heaven to Peter and his successors. However, the Pope is not impeccable. Infallibility is immunity from error under certain circumstances. Impeccability is immunity from sin. The Pope can commit sin in his personal life, but when he acts in his capacity as Pope, he is preserved free from error when he exercises his full teaching authority.

Why can't I pick and choose?

I don't have the right to be a "cafeteria Catholic," picking and choosing what teachings I will accept and obey. Teachings of the Church are authoritative and binding even if they do not include an "infallible definition" or a "definitive" pronouncement, when they "propose in the exercise of the ordinary

Magisterium a teaching that leads to better understanding of Revelation in matters of faith and morals."[8] These exercises of the ordinary Magisterium (or teaching authority, from the Latin word, "magister," or "teacher") must be accepted by Catholics in the formation of their consciences. "To this ordinary teaching the faithful 'are to adhere to it with religious assent' which, though distinct from the assent of faith, is nonetheless an extension of it."[9] "Bishops who teach in communion with the Roman Pontiff," said the Second Vatican Council, "are to be revered by all as witnesses of divine and Catholic truth; the faithful . . . are obliged to submit to their bishops' decision, made in the name of Christ, in matters of faith and morals, and to adhere to it with a ready and respectful allegiance of mind. This loyal submission of the will and intellect must be given in a special way, to the authentic teaching authority of the Roman Pontiff, even when he does not speak *ex cathedra*, in such wise, indeed, that his supreme teaching authority be acknowledged with respect, and that one sincerely adhere to decisions made by him, conformably with his manifest mind and intention."[10]

The Canon Law of the Church provides that, "each and everything set forth definitively by the Magisterium . . . regarding teaching on faith and morals must be firmly accepted and held; . . . therefore, anyone who rejects propositions which are to be held definitively sets himself against the teaching of the Catholic Church."[11] The teaching condemning euthanasia or providing that priestly ordination is reserved only to men are examples of such definitive teachings.[12] Moreover, teachings that are not proclaimed definitively must still be obeyed.

> While the assent of faith is not required, a religious submission of intellect and will is to be given to any doctrine which either the Supreme Pontiff or the College of Bishops, exercising their authentic Magisterium, declare upon a matter of faith and morals, even though they do not intend to proclaim that doctrine by definitive act. Christ's faithful are therefore to ensure that they avoid whatever does not accord with that doctrine.[13]

The teaching by Pope John Paul II on the use of the death penalty, for example, may or may not be "definitive." But that makes no difference because it still obliges Catholics according to the terms of Canon 752, quoted immediately above.

Why can't I be Pope?

Some Catholics claim to reject the teachings of the Church on, say, contraception or abortion, because those teachings have not been defined infallibly, *ex cathedra*. What those persons are really saying is that they prefer their own private judgment to that of the Pope. Everyone has a pope, that is, a moral authority that that person recognizes and obeys. The Catholic Church affirms that the authoritative moral teacher is the successor of Peter, who today is Benedict XVI. If a Catholic rejects the real Pope as his pope, he has to find another one. Inevitably it will end up being himself. Such "dissenting" Catholics are essentially Protestants.

Protestants reject the teaching authority of the Pope and of the Church on the ground that "the Bible is my infallible guide." But this makes no sense:

> Either such a person is infallibly certain that his . . . interpretation of the Bible is the correct one, or he is not. If he maintains that he is infallibly certain, then he claims for himself a personal infallibility. Furthermore, he cannot logically deny his personal infallibility to every other reader of the Bible. He denies it only to the Pope. We claim it only for the Pope. According to this view, each of the hundreds of millions of readers of the Bible becomes a pope while the only one who is not a pope is the Pope himself. . . . If one who holds this theory does not claim to be infallibly certain that his interpretation of the whole Bible is correct, then of what value is it to have an infallible Bible without an infallible interpreter? In either case the statement crumbles. . . .

> [A]n infallible Bible without an infallible living inter-
> preter is largely futile.[14]

If Christ meant the Bible to be our only guide, would he not have said so? He did not. And nowhere in the Bible will we find it said that the Bible is the only source of divine truth. Rather, that divine truth is found in "Sacred Tradition and Sacred Scripture."[15] What is Scripture? "Sacred *Scripture* is the speech of God as it is put down in writing under the breath of the Holy Spirit. And [Holy] *Tradition* transmits in its entirety the Word of God which has been entrusted to the apostles by Christ the Lord and the Holy Spirit."[16] What is Tradition? "Tradition . . . comes from the apostles and hands on what they received from Jesus' teaching and example and what they learned from the Holy Spirit. The first generation of Christians did not yet have a written New Testament, and the New Testament itself demonstrates the process of living Tradition."[17]

Again, *everyone* has a pope, in the sense that everyone recognizes an authoritative interpreter of the meaning of the moral law. If that interpreter is not the real Pope, it will be a pope of the individual's own selection: Time magazine, CNN, CBS News, the majority of the Supreme Court, or the individual himself. There can be only one Pope, not 6 billion. The institution of the papacy is one of God's great gifts, permitting us to be certain that the teachings we follow are God's own Truth.

The Church teaches on matters of faith and morals. An example of a teaching on faith is the teaching on the Real Presence of Christ in the Holy Eucharist. An example of a teaching on morals is the teaching on the objective evil of contraception. The primary focus of this book is on morals. Here, God has given us the natural moral law, which is a rule of reason. But we sometimes make mistakes in our application of the principles of the natural law. The teaching Church is given to us by God to provide reliable and certain answers on moral questions. In forming my conscience, I am bound to assent to the teachings of the Church on the issue involved. In one of his last published statements, on December 4, 2004, Pope John Paul II reminded visiting American bishops of "the Church's binding obligation to remind the faithful of their duty in conscience to act in accordance with her authoritative teaching."[18]

Endnotes

1 Gilbert K. Chesterton, *Orthodoxy* (New York: Dodd, Mead, 1946), 268–69.

2 *Matt*hew 28:19–20.

3 Trese, *The Faith Explained*, 121.

4 *Lumen Gentium*, nos. 22–25.

5 Trese, *The Faith Explained*, 141.

6 *Lumen Gentium*, no. 25; see *CCC*, no. 891.

7 *Lumen Gentium.*, no. 22.

8 *CCC*, no. 892.

9 *CCC*, no. 892, quoting *Lumen Gentium*, no. 25.

10 *Lumen Gentium*, no. 25.

11 Canon 750(2), as amended by Apostolic Letter *Ad Tuendam Fidem*, May 28, 1998.

12 Cardinal Joseph Ratzinger, "Commentary on Profession of Faith's Concluding Paragraphs," no. 11; 28 *Origins* (July 16, 1998), 116, 118–19; see *Inside the Vatican* (Aug.-Sept. 1998): 26, 27.

13 *Canon* 752.

14 Edward J. Hayes, Paul J. Hayes, and James J. Drummey, *Catholicism and Reason* (Our Sunday Visitor, 1990), 134–35.

15 *CCC*, no. 80, quoting *Dei Verbum*, no. 9.

16 *CCC*, no. 81, quoting *Dei Verbum*, no 9.

17 *CCC*, no. 83. See discussion of the development of the New Testament in James J. Drummey, *Catholic Replies* (Norwood, Mass.: C.R. Publications, 1995), 33–35.

18 50 *The Pope Speaks* (March/April 2005): 121–22.

14. THE NATURAL LAW?
WHAT'S THAT ALL ABOUT?

I have to make the same choice as Adam and Eve: to obey or disobey God. But what about those who have never heard of Christ and his Church and perhaps have never even heard of God? Do they have any hope of making it to heaven? The answer is: Yes. God gives to all men sufficient grace to be saved:

> "Since Christ died for all, . . . the Holy Spirit offers to all the possibility of being made partakers, . . . of the Paschal mystery." Every man who is ignorant of the Gospel of Christ and of his Church, but seeks the truth and does the will of God in accordance with his understanding of it, can be saved. It may be supposed that such persons would have *desired Baptism explicitly* if they had known its necessity.[1]

Such persons can be saved by baptism of desire, and they will be judged according to the natural law. Everything has a law of its nature, built into it by its maker. Thus a rock will sink if I throw it into a pond. "Natural law," however, means the law built into the nature of human beings, rational creatures made in the image and likeness of God. Saint Paul referred to this natural law when he said, "When the Gentiles who have no law do by nature what the Law prescribes. . . . [t]hey show the work of the Law written in their hearts."[2]

As Saint Thomas Aquinas (1225–1274) taught, there are four kinds of law: the eternal law, the divine law, the natural law, and the human law.

1. The eternal law

The world is not a product of chance. It was created by a loving God who has a purpose for me and for the world. A "universal rational orderliness" is "characteristic of the whole universe."[3] The "whole community of the universe is governed by Divine Reason. Wherefore the very Idea of the government of things in God the Ruler of the universe, has then the nature of a law."[4]

2. The divine law

Just as the maker of an automobile builds into it a certain nature (it is a vehicle, it drives, it does not fly) and gives directions for its use so that it will achieve its end, that is, dependable transportation, so God has built a certain nature into man and has given me directions to follow if I am to achieve my final end, which is eternal happiness with God in heaven. These directions are found, first, in the natural law, discussed in the next section of this chapter. That natural law is a knowable "rule of reason" built into the nature of human beings by which I can know what I ought to do to achieve my salvation. But, in addition to that natural law which I can discover by reason, God gave me specific directions, in Revelation, to help me know, without any doubt, what I ought to do. That Revelation is found in the Old Testament and the New Testament, which Saint Thomas calls the "divine law." Revelation also includes Tradition as handed down from the Apostles.[5]

The divine law is necessary, among other reasons, because, in Saint Thomas' words, "on account of the uncertainty of human judgment . . . different people form different judgments on human acts; whence also different and contrary laws result. In order, therefore, that man may know without any doubt what he ought to do and what he ought to avoid, it was necessary for man to be directed in his proper acts by a law given by God, for it is certain that such a law cannot err."[6] Although the obligations described in the Ten Commandments are "accessible to reason alone,"[7] God spelled them out in the Commandments because "sinful humanity needed this revelation." This was so because "in the state of sin . . . the light of reason was obscured and the will had gone astray."[8]

God, our Creator, not only gave us, in the Ten Command-ments, directions as to "man's fundamental duties towards God and towards his neigh-bor."[9] He also gave us an authoritative interpreter of those directions. That inter-preter is the teaching Church which is the "Mystical Body" of Christ.[10] As the Second Vatican Council said, "the task of giving an authentic interpre-tation to the Word of God, whether in its written form or in the form of Tradition, has been  entrusted to the living teaching office of the Church alone."[11] "Sacred Scripture is the speech of God as it is put down in writ-ing under the breath of the Holy Spirit."[12] "Tradition" is the "liv-ing transmission'" through which "the Church, in her doctrine, life, and worship . . . transmits to every generation all that she herself is, all that she believes."[13] The teaching office of the Church, to which both Scripture and Tradition are entrusted, is exercised by the Pope and the Bishops in union with the Pope.[14]

3. The natural law

At Reichsfuhrer Heinrich Himmler's suggestion, Dr. Karl Gebhardt, a Nazi physician at the SS hospital at

Hohenlychen, specialized in heteroplastic transplantation experiments. If an SS soldier had lost an arm or a leg, a replacement limb would be amputated from a live prisoner at the Ravensbrueck concentration camp. The prisoner would be killed in the process and his limb would be rushed to Dr. Gebhardt who would make the futile attempt to attach it to the SS amputee. Dr. Gebhardt was convicted at Nuremberg and hanged in 1948.[15]

Dr. Gebhardt's experiments were legal under the law of Nazi Germany. But were they right? Of course not. I can know right from wrong because, as Aquinas put it, man, as a rational creature, "has a share of the Eternal Reason. . . . [T]his partipation of the eternal law in the rational creature is called the natural law."[16] By "the light of natural reason . . . we discern what is good and what is evil. . . . [T]his is the function of the natural law."[17] The Gebhardt experiments violated that rule of reason, promulgated by God in man's nature. "[T]he natural law," said John Paul II, "is itself the eternal law, implanted in beings endowed with reason and inclining them towards their right action and end."[18] The Ten Commandments, also called the Decalogue or "ten words,"[19] contain "a privileged expression of the natural law. It is made known to us by divine revelation and by human reason."[20]

What are the commands of this natural law and how are they known? Again, as in Chapter 3, the key is to distinguish the speculative reason from the practical reason. The object of the speculative reason is being, while the object of the practical reason is the good. The first principle of the speculative reason is the principle of non-contradiction, that a thing cannot be and not be at the same time under the same aspect. That principle is self-evident; no rational person can doubt it.[21] In terms of its penness, a pen cannot be a pen and not be a pen.

The first self-evident principle of the practical reason is that "good is that which all things seek after."[22] All things, and not just human beings, seek the good, which is that which is in accord with their nature. That is why the grass grows up through the cracks in the sidewalk. And that is why I eat, sleep, and work out, because those things are good for me.

This first principle of the practical reason is the basis of the first, self-evident, principle of the natural law, that "good is to be done and pursued and evil is to be avoided."[23] Evil is not itself a thing but rather is "the privation," or absence, "of some particular good."[24]

The good is that which is in accord with the nature of the thing in question. Thus, it is good for me to eat a ham sandwich, but a barbed-wire sandwich is not good for me because my human stomach is not a trash compactor. Similarly, it is good to put gasoline in the tank of an automobile as needed. It is not good to put sand in the tank because the nature of an automobile is such that it is not made to run on sand. In the same way, chastity, according to my state in life, is good, but premarital sex or adultery is not. And so on.

Since the good is to be sought and evil is to be avoided, and since the good is that which is in accord with nature, the next obvious question is: What is the nature of man? The essential nature of man is unchangeable, since it is a reflection of the unchanging divine essence.[25] As Saint Thomas says, "all those things to which man has a natural inclination are naturally apprehended by reason as being good, and consequently as objects of pursuit, and their contraries as evil, and objects of avoidance."[26]

There are five basic natural inclinations of man:

1. To seek the good, which includes ultimately his highest good which is eternal happiness.

2. To preserve himself in existence.

3. To preserve the species, that is, to unite sexually and to have and care for children.

4. To live in community with other men.

5. To use his intellect and will, that is, to know the truth and to make his own decisions.[27]

But how do I decide?

God put these inclinations into human nature to help man achieve his final end of eternal happiness. From these inclinations I can reason by deduction to arrive at specific conclusions. I can use the syllogism: Good should be done; this action is good; this action therefore should be done.[28] Thus I can reason to the conclusion that theft is wrong because it violates the inclination to live in community. What kind of community would I live in if it were open season on cars in the parking lot and anyone could take my car whenever he so chose? Or if anyone could take any book he wanted from a public library and never return it?

The natural law is unchangeable in its general principles, but its application may vary in particular cases. A conclusion of the natural law – namely the inclination to live in community – is that when I borrow something I should return it to the lender. But if I discover that the person who lent me a baseball bat wants it back so he can murder someone, I am obliged not to return it to that lender because that would be immoral cooperation in his sin.[29]

But suppose I thought it was good when I did it?

Because of "concupiscence or some other passions . . . evil perversions . . . or . . . vicious customs and corrupt habits," people may come to the wrong conclusions in understanding or applying the secondary principles of the natural law.[30] For example, among some people, as Saint Thomas points out, homosexual activity was not considered sinful although he describes it as "the unnatural crime."[31]

An act contrary to the natural law, however, is always objectively wrong whether or not the person committing it is subjectively culpable. Everything has a nature, built into it by its maker, regardless of what I think of it. No matter how sincerely I may believe that sand in the gas tank is good for the car, the nature of the car is such that sand is not good for it. My subjective perception cannot change the objective law of the nature of the car. I may fervently desire and expect the car to run on sand, but it will not. Or I may sincerely believe that the brick will float, but when I throw it into the lake, I am bound to be disappointed. Or I may really think that premarital sex or adultery will make me happy, and I will find out that I am wrong.

The natural law is merely the story of how things work. If I want my car to work I must follow the laws built into its nature by its maker. The natural law "is . . . engraved in the soul of each and every man, because it is human reason ordaining him to do good and forbidding him to sin."[32] It "shows man the way to follow so as to practice the good and attain his end."[33] The Ten Commandments are specifications of the "principal precepts" of the natural law.[34] If I want to be happy and to achieve my purpose in life, I should follow those directions.

But am I to blame for it?

If I do what is objectively wrong, I am culpable for it if I know it is wrong and choose to do it. Even if my subjective culpability is reduced or eliminated by circumstances, the act remains objectively wrong. I can see this principle in the operation of the criminal law. John Hinckley, who attempted to assassinate President Reagan in 1981, committed an objective wrong. Whether he was subjectively culpable for it – that is, whether he was to blame and would be punished for it – depended on his knowledge and will. Did he know the assassination attempt was wrong and did he choose to do it with the necessary intent? His trial in 1982 ended in a verdict of not guilty by reason of insanity.[35] The law excused him from punishment as a criminal because he was insane. But if he were not insane, it would have been no excuse for him to say that, although he knew it was against the law, he sincerely believed that the President should be shot. So it is with the natural moral law. If I commit an objectively wrong act – whether theft, murder, impurity, or whatever else – I will be culpable if I know it is wrong and deliberately choose to do it.

Regardless of our subjective opinions, some acts are always objectively contrary to the natural law. If a friend asked me whether he should put molasses or oil into the crankcase of his car, would I ask him, "How do you *feel* about it?" Of course not. I would tell him it is not good for the car to put molasses into the crankcase, and I would try to convince him of that reality. So if a friend asks me whether he should commit a theft, fornication, or other immoral act, I have a duty to tell him that it is wrong and to try to convince him of that fact. I am not judging his subjective culpability. That is for God and the priest, hearing his confession, to decide. But I cannot fake reality. The reality is that some things are always wrong no matter what I, or someone else, may think of them.

One purpose of this book is to help us see how the teaching Church can help us to understand what the natural law requires. Obedience to the law of God can advance that understanding. Through his "choice of specific actions," man is "capable of giving his life direction and of following God's call."[36] "It is the 'heart' converted to the Lord and to the love of what is good which is really the source of *true* judgment of conscience. . . . This is the meaning of Jesus' saying: 'He who does what is true comes to the light.'"[37]

Habitual sin, on the other hand, can reduce the ability of our reason to make correct applications of the natural law. "[T]he systematic violation of the moral law," said John Paul II, "produces a . . . progressive darkening of the capacity to discern God's living and saving presence."[38]

But are there no exceptions?

One of the basic inclinations of human nature is to live in community. We know that this inclination is good. Through the natural law we know that we ought to promote the common good of the community and we ought to avoid what would detract from it. The "common good is . . . 'the sum total of social conditions which allow people, either as groups or as individuals, to reach their fulfillment more fully and more easily.'"[39] The common good requires respect for the person, social well-being and development, and peace.[40] Even our private acts can affect that common good. "[T]he natural law . . . is universal . . . and its authority extends to all mankind. . . . By submitting to the common law, our acts build up the true communion of persons. . . . When on the contrary they disregard the law, or even are merely ignorant of it, whether culpably or not, our acts damage the communion of persons, to the detriment of each."[41] This means that our immoral actions, even private ones, damage the common good by depriving the community of the moral persons we ought to be. The solitary and private drunk, for example, may not do anything overtly harmful. But he diminishes the community by depriving it of the person he should be. But, as Saint Thomas Aquinas taught and John Paul II agrees, the human law should not try to enforce every virtue or forbid every vice. As Aquinas said, the law must forbid those things without the prohibition of which the community could not be maintained, e.g., "murder, theft and suchlike."[42]

The "positive precepts" of the natural law, such as to serve and worship God and "to honor one's parents as they deserve," are "universally binding [and] unchanging."[43] But there can be exceptions, where the positive obligation yields to a higher duty or prohibition. If my parents order me to steal, I should not obey.

"The negative precepts of the natural law," however, permit no exception. They "oblige . . . always and in every circumstance."[44] "Thou shalt not commit adultery" for example, means "never"; it admits of no exception. Those negative precepts are as absolutely binding as a car manufacturer's negative command: "Thou shalt not put molasses in the crankcase." The negative commands of the natural law, including the specific prohibitions of the Commandments, as John Paul said in *Veritatis Splendor*, "forbid a given action *semper et pro semper* without exception, because the choice of this kind of behavior is in no case compatible with the goodness of the will of the acting person, with his vocation to life with God and to communion with his neighbor. . . . [M]an . . . can be hindered from doing certain good actions; but he can never be hindered from not doing certain actions, especially if he is prepared to die rather than to do evil. The Church has always taught that one may never choose kinds of behavior prohibited by the moral commandments expressed in negative form in the Old and New Testaments."[45]

The Ten Commandments are a specification of the natural law. Theft is forbidden. But first, following Church teaching, we have to define the crime. Because of the universal destination of goods, it may not be theft for the starving man to take a loaf of bread from one who has plenty.[46] If an act is really theft, we must *never* do it.

The Moral Act: In Summary

"Human acts, that is, acts that are freely chosen in consequence of a judgment of conscience . . . are either good or evil."[47] Whether an act is good or evil depends on:

1. *The object chosen. What* am I doing? As discussed above, you are free to make choices. But some things are intrinsically evil and it is always wrong to choose to do them.

2. *The end in view or the intention. Why* am I doing it? What is my purpose in doing it?

3. *The circumstances,* including the consequences that are likely to result from my act. I choose to rob a bank. My purpose is to pay off my credit cards. The circumstances are that I don't have other income to pay them off. It is wrong for me to rob that bank. *The bottom line:* Neither a good purpose nor the circumstances can justify an intrinsically wrong action. A good end does not justify a bad means. On the other hand, a bad purpose can make evil an act that would otherwise be good. To give money to charity is a good thing. But if my purpose in giving it is to embarrass another person who cannot give, then the act of giving becomes evil. "A *morally good* act requires

the goodness of the object, of the end, and of the circumstances together."[48]

Laying it on the line

The story of Captain James Mulligan, of the United States Navy, brings the natural law out of the abstract. After his plane was shot down in 1966, Captain Mulligan spent seven years in North Vietnamese prisons, half of them in solitary confinement. After his release, he described how his faith sustained him throughout his ordeal. His daily ritual was "permeated with prayer." He prayed the Rosary every day, counting the Hail Marys on the barbs on the wire fence of the prison. He laid it on the line and prayed: "Lord, give me the strength and the guts to see this thing through to the end, one way or another. No one else knows, Lord, but you and I know, and that's all that's necessary. You suffered for your beliefs, and I must suffer for mine. Right is right if no one's right; wrong is wrong if everyone's wrong."[49]

What's the bottom line on the natural law? Capt. Mulligan sums it up: "Right is right if no one's right; wrong is wrong if everyone's wrong."

4. The human law

This is the fourth kind of law. Saint Thomas defines law, in general, as "An ordinance of reason for the common good, made by him who has care of the community, and promulgated."[50] The human law is the law made by the state or other human lawgiver. The human law and its relation to the higher divine and natural laws are covered in later chapters of this book.

Endnotes

1 *CCC*, no. 1260 quoting *Gaudium et Spes*, no. 22; citing *Lumen Gentium* 16; *Ad Gentes* 7.

2 *Romans* 2:14–15.

3 Anton-Hermann Chroust, "The Philosophy of Law of St. Thomas Aquinas," 17 *American Journal of Jurisprudence* (1974): 1, 24.

4 *ST*, I, II, Q, 91, art. 1.

5 *CCC*, nos. 75–79.

6 *ST,* I, II, Q. 91, art. 4.

7 *CCC*, no. 2071.

8 *CCC*, no. 2071, quoting Saint Bonaventure, *Comm. Sent.* 4, 37, 1, 3.

9 *CCC*, no. 2072.

10 *CCC*, no. 791.

11 *Dei Verbum*, no. 10.

12 *CCC*, no. 81, quoting *Dei Verbum*, no. 9.

13 *CCC*, no. 78, quoting *Dei Verbum*, no. 8.

14 See Chapters 12 and 13 of this book.

15 Charles E. Rice, "Twisting Fate with 'Medicine,'" *The Observer* (Notre Dame, Ind., Sept. 9, 2004): 10; see also, Leo Alexander, M.D., "Medical Science Under Dictatorship," 241 *New England Journal of Medicine* (1949): 39.

16 *ST*, I, II, Q. 91, art. 2.

17 *Ibid.*, art. 1.

18 *VS*, no. 44.

19 *CCC*, no. 2056, citing *Exodus* 34:28 and *Deuteronomy* 4:13; 10:4.

20 *CCC*, no. 2080.

21 See Chapter 3 of this book.

22 *ST*, I, II, Q. 94, art. 2.

23 *Ibid.*

24 Saint Thomas Aquinas, *On Evil*, Q. 1, art. *1* (John and Jean Oesterle translation, Notre Dame, Ind. University of Notre Dame Press, 1995).

25 Heinrich Rommen, *The Natural Law* (Indianapolis, Ind.: Liberty Fund, 1998), 39–45.

26 *ST,* I, II, Q. 94, art. 2.

27 See Saint Thomas Aquinas, *ST*, I, II, Q. 94 art. 2; Thomas E. Davitt, s.j., "St. Thomas Aquinas and the Natural Law," in *Origins of the Natural Law Tradition* (Dallas: Southern Methodist Univ. Press, 1954), 26, 30–31; Rommen, *The Natural Law*, 42–45.

28 Rommen, *The Natural Law*, 42–45.

29 *ST*, I, II, Q. 94, art. 4.

30 *Ibid.,* art. 6.

31 *Ibid.*, art. 3, art. 6.

32 *CCC*, no. 1954, quoting Leo XIII, *Libertas Praestantissimum*, 597.

33 *CCC*, no. 1955.

34 *Ibid.*

35 *New York Times* (Aug. 10, 1982): 1.

36 *VS,* no. 67.

37 *VS,* no. 64.

38 *EV,* no. 21.

39 *CCC*, no. 1906, quoting *Gaudium et Spes*, no. 26, §1.

40 *CCC*, nos. 1907–9.

41 *VS*, no. 51.

42 *ST*, I, II, Q. 96, art. 2.

43 *VS,* no. 52.

44 *Ibid.*

45 *Ibid.*

46 *CCC*, no. 2408, quoting Gaudium et Spes, no. 69, §1

47 *CCC*, no. 1749.

48 *CCC*, no. 1755; see *CCC*, 1749–61.

49 James Mulligan, *The Hanoi Commitment* (Virginia Beach, Va.: RIF Marketing, 1981), 48, 93–94.

50 *S.T.*, I, II, Q. 90, art. 4.

15. WHAT ABOUT MY CONSCIENCE?

But how do I know what is right? Shouldn't my conscience be my guide?

Our conscience is "a judgment of reason" by which we recognize the rightness or wrongness of a specific act.[1] That judgment may be influenced by emotion, but it is an act of the intellect, judging that: "This is good," or "This is bad." Conscience is not an act of our will by which we make an arbitrary choice.

The test is not how we "feel" about the act of impurity, or theft, or whatever. As we discussed in Chapter 1, we should not check our brains at the door. Rather, we have to use our heads, to judge, in accord with the Truth, whether an act is really good. It may not be good even though I "feel" like I want to do it.

"[C]onscience expresses itself in acts of 'judgment' which reflect the truth about the good and not in arbitrary decisions."[2]

"The judgment of conscience is a *practical judgment*, which makes known what man must do or not do, or which assesses an act already performed by him. It . . . applies to a concrete situation the rational conviction that one must love and do good and avoid evil."[3]

Conscience has an additional function. It acts as a sanction, applying our practical judgment about the morality of an action to us in a personal way. In addition to telling us that theft is wrong ("it would be wrong to steal this"), conscience also tells me, "I must not steal this!" or if I am considering whether or not to tell the truth, my conscience will tell me not only that it is right to tell the truth in general, but also that I must tell the truth *now*.

Finally, the conscience, when it is operating properly, also causes us to feel emotions of approval or disapproval over our actions. If we do something that is good, we normally feel happy and at peace with ourselves. If we do something that is objectively bad, we normally feel guilty. Remember, in Chapter 5 of this book, Cardinal Newman's argument that this impact of conscience proves the existence of a personal God. When we hear the voice of conscience, we hear the voice of God, the Supreme Judge. Guilt is often regarded as something negative, but our feelings of guilt after we have done wrong can be a tremendous benefit to us. In a 1991 workshop for American Bishops, Cardinal Joseph Ratzinger (who became Pope Benedict XVI) cited the work of psychologist Albert Gorres, in emphasizing that our ability to feel guilt forces us to confront the evil that we have done and prevents us from lying to ourselves about it:

> [T]he feeling of guilt, the capacity to recognize guilt, belongs essentially to the spiritual make-up of man. This feeling of guilt disturbs the false calm of conscience and could be called conscience's complaint against my self-satisfied existence. It is as necessary for man as the physical pain which signifies disturbances of normal bodily functioning. Whoever is no longer capable of perceiving guilt is spiritually ill, "a living corpse, an actor's mask," as Gorres says.
>
> No longer seeing one's guilt, the falling silent of conscience in so many areas, is an even more dangerous sickness of the soul than the guilt which one recognizes as such. He who no longer notices that killing is a sin has fallen further than the one who still recognizes the shamefulness of his actions, because the former is further removed from the truth and conversion. Not without reason does the self-righteous man in the encounter

with Jesus appear as the one who is really lost. . . . The
Pharisee no longer knows that he too has guilt. He has a
completely clear conscience. But this silence of conscience makes him impenetrable to God and men.[4]

What are my duties to my conscience?

As with other judgments we make, our judgment of conscience may be wrong. Whether we are culpable for that mistake
will depend on whether we have fulfilled three duties:

1. *Form it.* "Conscience is not an independent and exclusive
capacity to decide what is good and what is evil. Rather there
is . . . imprinted upon it a principle of obedience [to] the
objective norm . . . at the basis of human behavior."[5] This
means that conscience is our judgment as to whether a specific act will or will not be in accord with the objective moral
law. Conscience is not a god-like ability to determine what
the moral law is. Like any other judgment we make, the judgment of our conscience may be wrong. Our first duty to our
conscience is to take steps to form a correct judgment as to
whether the act will be right or wrong. This is similar to the
way we form other judgments we make.

If I were deciding what size tires to put on my car, I would
form that decision by looking at the owner's manual, the manufacturer's directions. So it is with the judgment of my conscience as to the moral rightness or wrongness of an act. My
first duty is to form that judgment by consulting the directions
of our divine Creator, who speaks to us through the natural law
and the teachings of the Church. Consider whether the act
would be consistent with the five basic inclinations we discussed in Chapter 14: To seek the good, to preserve oneself, to
preserve the species, to live in community, and to know and to
choose. Through reason we can arrive at the right answer. But
God has not left us to figure these things out with only our reason to guide us. "The Ten Commandments state what is
required in the love of God and love of neighbor."[6] The

Catechism numbers the Commandments according to the division established by Saint Augustine:[7]

1. I am the LORD your God; you shall not have strange Gods before me.
2. You shall not take the name of the LORD your God in vain.
3. Remember to keep holy the LORD's Day.
4. Honor your father and your mother.
5. You shall not kill.
6. You shall not commit adultery.
7. You shall not steal.
8. You shall not bear false witness against your neighbor.
9. You shall not covet your neighbor's wife.
10. You shall not covet your neighbor's goods.[8]

"Christians have a great help for the formation of conscience *in the Church and her Magisterium.* . . . 'In forming their consciences the Christian faithful must give careful attention to the . . . teaching of the Church. For the Catholic Church is by the will of Christ the teacher of truth. Her charge is to . . . teach . . . that truth which is Christ, and . . . to declare and confirm the principles of the moral order which derive from human nature itself.'"[9] I need the Church because "[c]onscience *is not an infallible judge*; it can make mistakes."[10]

2. *Follow it if it is clear and certain.* Our second duty is to follow the judgment of our conscience as to the rightness or wrongness of an act *if that judgment is clear and certain.* "Like the natural law itself and all practical knowledge, the judgment of conscience also has an imperative character; man must act in accordance with it."[11] If my judgment is objectively wrong, I may be culpable for failing to form my conscience properly. Obviously, if my conscience is clear and free from doubt, I should follow my conscience. But don't minimize our first duty to educate and form our own conscience. And don't overlook our third duty with respect to conscience.

3. *Never act on a doubtful conscience.* This duty is often over-looked. "If man acts against this judgment [of conscience] or, in a case where he lacks certainty about the rightness of [an] act, still performs that act, he stands condemned by his own conscience."[12] Suppose I work in an office. Can I use the office postage for my personal mail? Maybe on other occasions I spent my own money on office purposes for which I was not reimbursed. But I am still not sure it is right to run my personal mail through the office postage meter to recoup what I could have claimed for reimbursement but didn't. If I am in doubt as to whether a particular action is right and I choose to do it anyway, I am choosing to do what, for all I know, may be wrong. But I know I will not do wrong if I do not do the act. If in doubt, try to resolve the doubt. If the doubt persists, take the safer course. The *Catechism of the Catholic Church* offers rules to help us resolve such doubt:

> Man is sometimes confronted by situations that make moral judgments less assured and decision difficult. But he must always seriously seek what is right and good and discern the will of God expressed in divine law.

> To this purpose, man strives to interpret the data of experience and the signs of the times assisted by the virtue of prudence, by the advice of competent people, and by the help of the Holy Spirit and his gifts.

> Some rules apply in every case:
> • One may never do evil so that good may result from it;
> • The Golden Rule: "Whatever you wish that men would do to you, do so to them."
> • Charity always proceeds by way of respect for one's neighbor and his conscience: "Thus sinning against your brethren and wounding their conscience . . . you sin against Christ." Therefore "it is right not to . . . do anything that makes your brother stumble."[13]

It would be virtually impossible for a believing Catholic to think beyond any doubt that an action prohibited by a clear teaching of the Church, such as contraception, abortion, extramarital sex, etc., is right. Many Catholics will say, for example, "I disagree in conscience with the Church's teaching on contraception." Usually that means, "I think contraception is a permissible option." Let's follow that reasoning to its logical conclusion. He thinks that contraception is allowed but not required. He thinks he *may* practice contraception, *but is not obliged to do so.* If that is what he thinks, he can follow the Church's teaching and refrain from contraception without violating the judgment of his conscience. The only time a person's judgment as to the morality of his practicing contraception would precisely and inescapably conflict with the Church's teaching would be if that judgment of his conscience told him he *must* practice contraception. His judgment in that case would conflict with the teaching of the Church that "You *must not* practice contraception." But in that case, where a clear teaching of the Church prohibits contraception, it would be virtually inconceivable that a believing Catholic could think beyond any doubt that the prohibited action, i.e., contraception, was mandatory for him.

Remember that the Church is the Mystical Body of Christ, and the Pope, the successor of Peter, is the Vicar of Christ on earth. If my friend, Freddy, follows his own preference in contradiction to a clear teaching of the Church, then he is really saying that his pope is not Benedict XVI but Freddy I. We can't have it both ways. We have to pick our pope. If we claim to be a Catholic, we have to follow the real Pope, not one of our own invention.

How can I really be free?

In our culture, "[C]onscience is no longer considered . . . as an act of a person's intelligence . . . to express a judgment about the right conduct to be chosen here and now. Instead, there is a tendency to grant to the . . . conscience the prerogative of independently determining the criteria of good and evil."[14] It is a fact of life, however, that "when a man shows little concern for seeking what is true and good . . . conscience gradually becomes almost blind from being accustomed to sin."[15] What this culture rejects is the reality that "the frank and open acceptance of truth is the condition for authentic freedom."[16] I may feel free and uninhibited when I pour the molasses into the crankcase. But I will no longer be free to drive my car because I have acted contrary to the truth of its nature. With human beings, too, the natural law is the story of how things work. Conformity to the truth of our nature is the prerequisite for true freedom. As with the car, we do not determine what is in accord with our nature and what seriously violates that nature. God makes those determinations:

> God is the one who makes known, through reason and revelation, what constitutes a grave sin. Those who with full deliberation and consent commit adultery, murder, perjury and similar crimes estrange themselves from God. He sets down the conditions for their estrangement, not they. It is not up to man to decide subjectively whether a deliberate serious sin, like direct abortion, is also a mortal sin which derives him of God's friendship. The sinner cannot excuse himself of mortal sin by the clever distinction that psychologically "I do not really want to reject God. I only intend to do what I know God forbids as a serious violation of his law." God alone has the right to determine what separates a sinner from his Creator; a creature does not have the right to stand in judgment on God and tell him what constitutes a mortal sin.

> The Church's basic position on mortal sin, therefore, has not changed. Subjectively a person is guilty of mortal sin when he fully consents with his will to do what he realizes is a serious offense against God. Otherwise, although the matter is grave, if only partial consent was given then only venial sin was

committed. But the object of this consent is what God, and not man, determines is gravely wrong.

Consequently a venial sin is committed either when the matter (misdeed) is not objectively serious, and the circumstances do not make it serious; or when the matter is serious but full consent is not given by the free will.[17]

Our obligation to obey the Commandments applies across the board to all our actions. "The Ten Commandments, in their fundamental content, state grave obligations. However, obedience to these precepts also implies obligations in matter which is, in itself, light."[18]

Pope John Paul II described conscience as an "interior *dialogue of man with himself.* But it is also a *dialogue of man with God*, the author of the law. . . . [Conscience is] the sacred place where God speaks to man."[19] As John Paul put it, "Conscience is *the witness of God himself*, whose voice and judgment penetrate the depth of man's soul, calling him *fortiter et suaviter* (strongly yet gently) to obedience."[20]

Endnotes

1   *CCC*, no. 1778.

2   *VS*, no. 61.

3   *VS*, no. 59.

4   Cardinal Joseph Ratzinger, *Conscience and Truth*. Presented at the 10th workshop for bishops, Dallas, TX, February 1991. http://www.ewtn.com/library/CURIA/RATZCONS.HTM

5   *VS*, no. 60.

6   *CCC*, no. 2067.

7   *CCC*, no. 2066.

8   See *CCC*, no. 2052.

9   *VS*, no. 64.

10   *VS*, no. 62.

11   *VS*, no. 60.

12 *Ibid.*

13 *CCC*, nos. 1787–1789, quoting *Matthew* 7:12; *1 Corinthians* 8:12; *Romans* 14:21; citing *Luke* 6:31; *Tobit* 4:15.

14 *FR*, no. 98.

15 *VS*, no. 62.

16 *VS*, no. 87.

17 Hardon, *The Catholic Catechism*, 293–94.

18 *CCC*, no. 2081.

19 *VS*, no. 58.

20 *VS*, no. 64.

16. HOW DO I RELATE TO OTHERS?

What do you mean, "relate"?

The three persons in God have (or more precisely, are) a social life. As Aquinas put it, "relation in God . . . is the divine essence itself."[1] The essence of each divine person "includes the idea of relation" to the other divine persons.[2] "God is . . . eternally Father in relation to his only Son, who is eternally Son only in relation to his Father."[3] The Holy Spirit proceeds eternally from both the Father and the Son.[4] "The Holy Spirit . . . is God, one and equal with the Father and the Son, of the same substance and also of the same nature."[5] Since I am made in the image and likeness of God I am relational. As the Second Vatican Council said, "the Lord Jesus, when praying to the Father 'that they may also be one . . . even as we are one'[6] has opened up new horizons closed to human reason by implying that there is a certain parallel between the unity existing among the divine persons and the unity of the sons of God in truth and love. It follows, then, that if man is the only creature on earth that God has wanted for its own sake, man can fully discover his true self only in a sincere giving of himself."[7]

God didn't make us to be alone. He created each of us as part of a family, and as part of the whole human race. God could have made us live all by ourselves individually – he can do anything. But he didn't. Instead God chose to have each of us born to a mother and a father, with relatives and friends and neighbors. This is our *nature*. That is simple, but it's very important. It helps us to understand more about ourselves and how we should act toward others.

The Father, the Son, and the Holy Spirit are a communion of Persons who love each other. Since we are made in the image and likeness of the Trinity, we, too, exist in relation to others. Our relational nature doesn't end with our biological families.

Am I my brother's keeper?

"Cain said to Abel, his brother, 'Let us go out to the field.' And when they were in the field, Cain rose up against his brother Abel, and killed him. Then the Lord said to Cain, 'Where is Abel your brother?'" He said, "I do not know; am I my brother's keeper?'"[8]

"Yes," answered John Paul II, "every man is his 'brother's keeper,'" because God entrusts us to one another. . . . [I]n view of this entrusting . . . God gives everyone freedom, a freedom which possesses an inherently relational dimension. This is a great gift of the Creator, placed as it is at the service of the person and of his fulfillment through the gift of self and openness to others; but when freedom is made absolute in an individualistic way, it is emptied of its original content, and its very meaning and dignity are contradicted."[9] Thus Benedict XVI, in his New York address to youth, warned against "a poisoned attitude of mind which results in people being treated as mere objects." Instead, he encouraged the young people "to invite others, especially the vulnerable and the innocent, to join you along the way of goodness and hope."[10]

I am "my brother's keeper," not for an arbitrary reason, but because that relation to others is part of my nature. I am my brother's keeper simply because *that's the way I am.* Relationships carry responsibilities. Our primary duties are to our families, our closest relatives. Each person has a responsibility to love and obey his parents, to love and care for his own children, and to love and respect other family members. If we fail to live up to our responsibilities to others, they suffer. But so do we. That failure will harm us as well.

How do we live up to those responsibilities? We do it by cultivating habits. We are creatures of habit – with repetition, an act becomes easier and easier to perform. Suppose I decide that every day I am going to get up an hour earlier than I had been getting up. At first I may have difficulty waking up and getting out of bed, but after a few days, I will find that I am waking up at this earlier time every day. I develop moral habits, good and bad, as well. A habit of doing something good is a virtue, while a habit of doing something evil is a vice. When we tell lies to others, it becomes easier to lie, and soon we develop the vice of dishonesty. If we always tell the truth to others even when it is difficult to do so, we develop the virtue of honesty. When we work at acquiring virtues, we fulfill our nature. When we drift into habits of vice, we violate that nature – to our detriment.

The virtues and vices that we develop as a result of the actions we choose to do will make us a better or a worse person and will affect how we treat other people. Two sets of virtues – the cardinal and the theological – are especially important. They help us to treat other people with the dignity and respect that they deserve.

The Cardinal Virtues –
prudence, justice, fortitude, and temperance

The cardinal moral virtues – prudence, justice, fortitude, and temperance – are called that from the Latin, cardo, or hinge, because they are virtues on which the other moral virtues hinge or depend.

Prudence. This virtue helps us "to discern our true good in every circumstance and to choose the right means of achieving it."[11] As *Proverbs* put it, "the prudent man looks where he is going."[12] Prudence is a practical virtue. If I want to go to college, for example, it is prudent to study hard in high school and to take college preparatory courses. But prudence is important also in our relationships with other people. If I decide that I want to give my old clothes to one of my friends whose family is poor, it is prudent to give them to her privately to avoid embarrassing her.

If I give them to her in front of my friends, or announce to everyone that I am happy to see her wearing my old clothes, I will probably have one less friend. Inevitably, we make mistakes of imprudence as we are growing up.

Prudence is proper to my nature, especially because it is "*auriga virtutum* (the charioteer of the virtues); it guides the other virtues by setting rule and measure."[13] But we are not born with prudence – we learn to be prudent by working at it in cooperation with God's grace. Prudence "is not to be confused with timidity or fear, nor with duplicity or dissimulation. . . . With the help of this virtue we apply moral principles to particular cases without error and overcome doubts about the good to achieve and the evil to avoid."[14]

Justice. This virtue "consists in the constant and firm will to give their due to God and neighbor."[15] This doesn't just mean returning things we borrowed, or paying money we owe people. When we act justly we acknowledge that others have human rights and treat them in accord with their nature and supernatural destiny. For example, justice requires that we recognize someone else's right to life and act accordingly. Justice requires that we recognize someone else's right to a just wage and pay him accordingly. Justice requires that we treat each person with the dignity and respect owed to him as a child of God.

Fortitude. This virtue "ensures firmness in difficulties and constancy in the pursuit of the good. It strengthens the resolve to resist temptations and to overcome obstacles in the moral life. . . . [It] enables one to conquer fear, even fear of death, and to face trials and persecutions."[16] We may think of fortitude as the virtue that helps us do brave things, but there is another aspect. Fortitude helps us to endure difficulties and to be patient so we can do what we should. A person of fortitude will be kind to the neighborhood pest no matter what others might say. A person with fortitude will bravely stand up for the rights of others, even when threatened with personal or financial penalties. Many pro-life leaders have been threatened with lawsuits for organizing protests at abortion clinics. Everyone who peacefully prays at abortion clinics has had the experience of being harassed and ridiculed. Fortitude enables them to continue their pro-life work, even when it is difficult.

Temperance. This is "the moral virtue that moderates the attraction of pleasures and provides balance in the use of created goods."[17] Temperance helps us to control our own desires for pleasures. Why is this important? Without temperance we will become so attached to those pleasures that we will ignore our own good. Every year some college students die from alcohol poisoning or other consequences of their drinking more alcohol than their bodies can handle. Or a lack of temperance can cause us to ignore someone else's needs and sufferings. The virtue of temperance enables us to recognize when someone else has a need that should come before our own desires. As with other virtues, we can cultivate the habit of temperance in little things. We act temperately whenever we limit ourselves to one piece of dessert so that there is enough for others, when we clean out our closets and give away what we don't need, or when we give money to the poor instead of buying something we don't need. Our own self-control and detachment from our desires helps other people, and we become a better person in the process.

The Theological Virtues – faith, hope, and charity

The cardinal virtues are important for treating others well, but they are not enough. We am called to a higher standard – to love as Jesus does, in accord with our nature as children of God created in his image and likeness. To do this we need the supernatural virtues of faith, hope, and charity.

The cardinal, or human, virtues "are rooted in the theological virtues . . . [which] dispose Christians to live in a relationship with the Holy Trinity. . . . The theological virtues are the foundation of Christian moral activity. . . . They . . . give life to all the moral virtues. . . . There are three theological virtues: faith, hope and charity."[18] The theological virtues "have God for their origin, their motive, and their object – God known by faith, God hoped in and loved for his own sake."[19]

Faith "[W]e believe in God and believe all that he has said and revealed to us, and that Holy Church proposes for our belief, because he is truth itself."[20]

Hope "[W]e desire . . . heaven and eternal life as our happiness, placing our trust in Christ's promises and relying not on our own strength, but on the help of the grace of the Holy Spirit."[21]

Charity "[W]e love God above all things for his own sake, and our neighbour as ourselves for the love of God."[22]

In his first encyclical, Deus Caritas Est (God is Love) (DCE), Pope Benedict XVI spoke of "the love which God lavishes upon us and which we in turn must share with others."[23] "Love of God and love of neighbor have become one: in the least of the brethren we find Jesus himself and in Jesus we find God."[24] DCE includes an explanation of "Caritas," the "practice" of love of neighbor. "[N]o one ought to go without the necessities of life."[25] That "service of charity" is "first and foremost a responsibility for each . . . member of the faithful" but it is also a duty of the Church at every level.[26]

"Christian charity" is not abstract. It is "first of all the . . . response to immediate needs . . . : feeding the hungry, clothing the naked, caring for . . . the sick, visiting those in prison, etc." But people "need something more than technically proper care. . . . They need heartfelt concern." Charity therefore cannot be "just another form of social assistance." Nor is charity a means of "proselytism," using aid to induce conversions. Charity is an act of love and "[l]ove is free; it is not practiced as a way of achieving other ends."[27]

Pope Benedict XVI's second encyclical "Spe Salvi," drew its title from its opening words, "'SPE SALVI facti sumus' – in hope we were saved." The message is simple: "A world without God is a world without hope."[28] A secularist culture, Benedict insists, can offer no hope for anything after death. No future. In contrast, their "encounter with Christ" gives Christians their "distinguishing mark" which is "the fact that they have a future: it is not that they know the details... but they know in general terms that their life will not end in emptiness. Only when the future is certain as a positive reality does it become possible to live the present as well."[29]

Benedict affirms the achievements and potential of science, but he cautions that "[i]f technical progress is not matched by . . . progress in man's ethical formation... it is not progress at all, but a threat for man and for the world."[30] The problem is that ethical formation is impossible unless reason can offer answers on moral right and wrong. But reason cannot do that if it is limited to the empirical, without "integration, through . . . openness . . . to the differentiation between good and evil . . . [R]eason . . . becomes human only if it is capable of directing the will along the right path and it is capable of this only if it looks beyond itself. . . . Let us put it very simply: man needs God, otherwise he remains without hope... God truly enters into human affairs only when, rather than being present merely in our thinking, he himself comes towards us and speaks to us.... Reason... and faith need one another in order to fulfill their true nature and their missions."[31]

Faith and hope enable us to put our relations with other human beings into the perspective of eternal life. Through faith, we believe what God tells us, not only about himself, but also about ourselves and how we should act toward him and others. Through hope, we long for eternal happiness for ourselves and for those whom we love. Charity enables us to love others sacrificially as Jesus did. "The Lord asks us to love as he does, even our *enemies*, to make ourselves the neighbor of those furthest away, and to love children and the poor as Christ himself."[32]

Charity motivates us to stand in solidarity with the poor and the unloved. If we have solidarity with others, we understand that their good is also our own good. We know that we cannot separate what is good for us from what is good for them. Charity calls us to be willing to sacrifice, to suffer, and even die for others, just as Jesus gave his life for us on the Cross. As Chapter 2 told, charity motivated Saint Maximilian Kolbe to give his life for a fellow prisoner at Auschwitz. Charity motivated Saint Margaret Clitherow, a wife and mother, 33 years old, who was sentenced to death in 1586 for hiding priests during the persecution of Catholics in England. Margaret refused to plead to the charge; she refused to request a trial because she was afraid that her family and friends would either sin by perjuring themselves to save her or would suffer guilt from having provided the evidence that convicted her. Because she refused to plead, she was executed by being "pressed to death." She was placed on a stone floor, with a stone the size of a fist under her back. A door was placed over her and weights were piled on the door, "seven or eight hundred weight at the least," crushing her to death. "She was about a quarter of an hour dying."[33] But her death, which she chose in order to save her family and friends, earned her a never-ending and total happiness with God (and, we trust, with those friends and family) in Heaven.

Am I my brother's keeper? What can that mean anyway?

In response to God's inquiries about Abel, Cain protested, "Am I my brother's keeper?" Every time we question our responsibilities toward others, ignore someone else's needs, or treat someone unjustly or uncharitably, we effectively ask the same question. The answer is the same for us as it was for Cain: "Yes! I am my brother's keeper." But it doesn't end there.

"By virtue of human solidarity," says the Compendium of the Social Doctrine of the Church, "each individual's sin in some way affects others."[34] When you commit any sin, you diminish yourself and you deprive others of the person you ought to be. In other words, there are no victimless crimes. *"Certain sins, moreover, constitute . . . a direct assault on one's neighbor. Such sins are known as social sins.* Social sin is every sin committed against the justice due in relations between individuals, between the individual and the community, and . . . between the community and the individual. Social too is every sin against the rights of the human person, starting with the right to life."[35] If a society attempts to legitimize sinful behavior in its customs and law, it creates what the Catechism describes as "structures of sin":

> [S]in makes men accomplices of one another and causes concupiscence, violence, and injustice to reign among them. Sins give rise to social situations and institutions that are contrary to the divine goodness. "Structures of sin" are the expression and effect of personal sins. They lead their victims to do evil in their turn. In an analogous sense, they constitute a "social sin."[36]

You are, of course, responsible for your actions. Your acts of virtue can make society more just. Your sinful acts contribute to an unjust society. Moreover, even if you do not participate in it, you bear some responsibility if you approve or support an injustice. A business owner with a factory in a country that allows forced child labor or even slave labor must make sure that he is not allowing those unjust practices. In our own country, those who support legalized abortion bear responsibility for the women and unborn children who are its victims. The bottom line: You can't support an unjust practice even if it is legal. And you are obliged to do what you reasonably can to correct that injustice, including your most powerful weapon, which is prayer.

We will never end "social sins" without personal conversions. But each of us can and must start by examining our own conscience to see how we have contributed to or participated in these structures of sin. In Chapter 21, we will discuss how unjust laws give rise to social structures of sin and what our own response should be to social sins. For now, keep in mind that we cannot escape our relation to others. Whether we know it or not, our life of virtue or of sin sets a good or bad example for those we know and for others who see how we live.

I've got friends in high places

Finally, being relational doesn't end when we die. As discussed above in Chapter 4, "[e]ach man receives his eternal retribution in his immortal soul at the very moment of his death, in a particular judgment that refers his life to Christ."[37] This particular judgment determines whether our ultimate destiny will be heaven[38] or hell, the chief punishment of which "is eternal separation from God, in whom alone man can possess the life and happiness for which he was created and for which he longs."[39] "God predestines no one to go to hell; for this, a willful turning away from God (a mortal sin) is necessary, and persistence in it until the end."[40] In addition to the Particular Judgment, the Last Judgment will occur "when Christ returns in glory."[41] It "will reveal even to its furthest consequences the good each person has done or failed to do during his earthly life."[42] "Then Christ will come 'in his glory, and all the angels with him. . . . Before him will be gathered all the nations, and he will separate them one from another as a shepherd separates the sheep from the goats, and he will place the sheep at his right hand, but the goats at the left. . . . and they will go away into eternal punishment, but the righteous into eternal life.'"[43]

"Heaven is the blessed community of all who are perfectly incorporated into Christ."[44] We hope and trust that at the end of our lives we will enjoy union with God and the company of the saints and angels in heaven. Even now we can enjoy a relationship with the saints and angels. "In the communion of Saints, 'a perennial link of charity exists between the faithful who have already reached their heavenly home, those who are expiating their sins in purgatory, and those who are still pilgrims on earth.

Between them there is, too, an abundant exchange of all good things.'"[45]

"The souls of the departed" in Purgatory, said Benedict XVI, "can . . . receive 'solace and refreshment' through the Eucharist, prayer and almsgiving. The belief that love can reach into the afterlife . . . has been a fundamental conviction of Christianity throughout the ages."[46]

We can and should pray for those who have died, and we also can seek the prayers and help of the saints, the angels, and especially Mary, who is the Mother of God and our mother. They are a source of friendship and consolation for those who seek their help. We truly have friends in high places!

Endnotes

1 *ST*, I, Q. 29, art. 4.

2 *Ibid.*

3 *CCC*, no. 240.

4 *CCC*, no. 246.

5 *CCC*, no. 245, quoting Council of Toledo XI (675).

6 *John* 17:21–22.

7 *Gaudium et Spes,* no. 24.

8 *EV,* no. 7, quoting *Genesis* 4:8–9.

9 *EV*, no. 19.

10 Pope Benedict XVI, Address to Youth, April 19, 2008.

11 *CCC*, no. 1806.

12 *Prov* 14:15, quoted in *CCC*, no. 1806.

13 *CCC*, no. 1806.

14 *Ibid.*

15 *CCC*, no. 1807.

16 *CCC*, no. 1808.

17 *CCC*, no. 1809.

18 *CCC*, nos. 1812, 1813, citing *2 Peter* 1:4; *1 Corinthians* 13:13.

19 *CCC*, no. 1840.

20 *CCC,* no. 1814.

21 *CCC*, no. 1817.

22   *CCC*, no. 1822.

23   Pope Benedict XVI, *Deus Caritas Est* (2005), no. 1.

24   DCE, no. 15.

25   *Ibid.*, no. 25.

26   *Ibid.*, no. 20.

27   *Ibid.*, no. 31.

28   Pope Benedict XVI, *Spe Salvi* (2007), no. 44.

29   *Ibid.*, no. 2.

30   *Ibid.*, no. 22

31   *Ibid.*, no. 23.

32   *CCC*, no. 1825, citing *Matthew* 5:44; *Luke* 10:27–37; *Mark* 9:37; *Matthew* 25:40, 45.

33   See generally, Margaret T. Monro, *St. Margaret Clitherow: The Pearl of York* (Rockford, Ill.: TAN Books, 2003), 54–63, 8edc

34   Pontifical Council for Justice and Peace, *Compendium of the Social Doctrine of the Church* (2005), No. 117, quoting John Paul II, *Reconciliatio et Paenitentia* (1985).

35   *Ibid.*, nos. 117–18.

36   *CCC*, no. 1869, quoting John Paul II, *Reconciliatio et Paenitentia* (1985).

37   *CCC*, no. 1022; see also no. 1051.

38   *CCC*, no. 1023.

39   *CCC*, no. 1035.

40   *CCC*, no. 1037, citing Council of Orange II (529) and Council of Trent (1547).

41   *CCC*, no. 1040.

42   *CCC*, no. 1039.

43   *CCC*, no 1038, quoting *Matthew* 25:31, 32, 46.

44   *CCC*, no. 1026.

45   *CCC*, no. 1475, quoting *Indulgentianum Doctrina*, no. 5.

46   *Spe Salvi*, no. 48

17. AM I A GIFT TO OTHERS?
WHAT ABOUT MY FREEDOM?

What about me?

So, it is important to see myself as a person in relation to God and to others, and, consequently, to act with justice and charity toward others. But, hold on: What about *me*? If I have free will, don't I get to do what I want? How can I be happy if I don't put my own needs first?

The answer may surprise us because we live in a culture that proclaims that the way to be happy is to think of ourselves first and put others second (a distant second at that). The culture believes that a person is an isolated individual who finds happiness by satisfying his own desires, even at the expense of others. We are, however, naturally created to live in community, so the answer is different from what we might expect.

Would Jesus agree?

Jesus Christ shows us, in the words of the Second Vatican Council, that "man can fully discover his true self only in a sincere giving of himself."[1] The perfect model for that self-gift is Jesus himself. "Following Christ," said John Paul II, "is not an outward imitation. . . . Being a follower of Christ means being conformed to him. . . . This is the effect of grace, of the active presence of the Holy Spirit in us."[2]

Later in this chapter we will learn what real freedom is. The "first necessary step on the journey toward freedom, its starting point," is to keep the Commandments, our Manufacturer's directions.[3] But if we want to go further, we must consider the Beatitudes:

> Blessed are the poor in spirit, for theirs is the kingdom of heaven.
>
> Blessed are those who mourn, for they shall be comforted.
>
> Blessed are the meek, for they shall inherit the earth.
>
> Blessed are those who hunger and thirst for righteousness, for they shall be satisfied.
>
> Blessed are the merciful, for they shall obtain mercy.
>
> Blessed are the pure in heart, for they shall see God.
>
> Blessed are the peacemakers, for they shall be called sons of God.
>
> Blessed are those who are persecuted for righteousness' sake, for theirs is the kingdom of heaven.
>
> Blessed are you when men revile you and persecute you and utter all kinds of evil against you falsely on my account.
>
> Rejoice and be glad,
>
> for your reward is great in heaven.[4]

"The Beatitudes are not specifically concerned with . . . particular rules of behavior. Rather, they speak of basic attitudes and dispositions in life."[5] They "teach us the final end to which God calls us: the Kingdom, the vision of God, participation in the divine nature, eternal life, filiation, rest in God."[6] Do we want to follow Christ? "The Beatitudes depict the countenance of Jesus Christ and portray his charity."[7] As John Paul II put it, "they are a sort of self-portrait of Christ and for this very reason are invitations to discipleship and communion of life with Christ."[8]

Our effort to be like Christ is aided by the gifts and fruits of the Holy Spirit. Those gifts are wisdom, understanding, counsel, fortitude, knowledge, piety and fear of the Lord. "They complete and perfect the virtues of those who receive them."[9] The fruits "are perfections that the Holy Spirit forms in us as the first fruits of eternal glory." They are charity, joy, peace, patience, kindness, goodness, generosity, gentleness, faithfulness, modesty, self-control and chastity.[10] Together with the cardinal and theological virtues, discussed in Question 16, the Holy Spirit has given these extra helps to enable us truly to model ourselves on Christ.

But will imitating Christ make me happy?

Isn't it true that the people who seem to be the happiest, who are at peace, are those who are generous and loving? In contrast, those who are most self-centered usually appear to be the least happy and never satisfied. This seems to be a paradox, but it isn't.

It makes sense because our nature is relational. God creates us to live in relation with himself and other human beings from the moment of our conception. We are born into a family, and as we grow up, "Jesus asks us to follow him and to imitate him along the path of love, a love which gives itself completely to the brethren out of love for God."[11]

Is this always easy? Well, no. I can see from Jesus' death on the cross that self-giving requires sacrificial love. It could even require us to lay down our lives for others. Through the grace of God, we will find our own happiness precisely in the giving of ourselves to others. Saint Gianna Beretta Molla, canonized by Pope John Paul II in 2004, was a wife, mother, and pediatrician. In 1961, when she was pregnant with her fourth child, doctors diagnosed a serious fibroma in her womb. The doctors recommended a morally permissible hysterectomy that would have saved her life but would have caused the death of her unborn child, but Gianna refused. She insisted instead on surgery to remove the tumor. "I shall accept whatever they will do to me," she said, "provided they save the child." The surgery, in September, 1961, removed the tumor and saved the unborn child, but the mother continued in perilous health. "If you must decide between me and the child," Gianna told her husband, "do not hesitate. Choose the child – I insist on it."

On April 20, 1962, Gianna went to the hospital to deliver her child. She was diagnosed to have a life-threatening septic peritonitis. On April 21, her daughter was born, But Gianna's health continued to decline. A week later, after repeatedly exclaiming, "Jesus, I love you. Jesus, I love you," Gianna died. After the earlier surgery, Gianna had "confessed impulsively to a visiting friend, 'I've suffered a lot, but I am happy because the pregnancy is saved.'" The child she saved grew up to become Dr. Gianna Emmanuela Molla. "[T]he witness of my mother," she said, "was a *hymn to life*, to a love for life and all the beautiful things in life. It was a hymn to a faith lived with joy and nourished by the Eucharist and by prayer."[12] In his homily at Saint Gianna's canonization Mass, John Paul II said:

> *Gianna Beretta Molla* was a simple, but more than ever, significant messenger of divine love. In a letter to her future husband a few days before their marriage, she wrote: *"Love is the most beautiful sentiment the Lord has put into the soul of men and women."* Following the example of Christ, who *"having loved his own . . . loved them to the end"* . . . this holy mother of a family remained heroically faithful to the commitment she made on the day of her marriage. The extreme sacrifice she sealed with her life testifies that only those who have the courage to give of themselves totally to God and to others are able to fulfill themselves. Through the example of Gianna Beretta Molla, may our age rediscover the pure, chaste and fruitful beauty of conjugal love, lived as a response to the divine call![13]

Gianna Beretta Molla was not unhappy with her decision. "The secret of happiness," she said, "is to live moment by moment and to thank God for all that He, in His goodness, sends to us day after day."[14]

Few people will be called by God to make the kind of sacrifice Saint Gianna made. But in small yet significant ways, being a gift to others requires us to sacrifice our own selfish desires for what is truly good. Every time I allow someone else to borrow something I wanted to use then myself, or I work at a soup kitchen instead of hanging out with friends, or I help out around the house, I am being a gift for others. No one can force us to do this, though. That is where our gift of freedom comes in.

Freedom – can't I do whatever I want?

One of the most effective tactics of abortion advocates is to call their movement "pro-choice" rather than "pro-abortion." Leaders in the abortion industry recognize that our culture exalts freedom, individual liberty, and choice above all. In this culture, the important thing is not what people choose, but choice itself. No moral difference is acknowledged between the choices people might make – instead, what matters is simply that they exercise the right to choose. The pro-abortion movement appeals to this belief by describing itself as promoting "choice" rather than abortion.

In effect, this belief holds that any choice we make is automatically right. Cardinal Joseph Ratzinger, in his homily to the Cardinals before the conclave in which they chose him to be Pope, said the "fashionable" attitude is "[a] dictatorship of relativism . . . that recognizes nothing as absolute and which only leaves the 'I' and its whims as the ultimate measure."[15] This attitude says we should just choose whatever we *feel* is right. We decide for ourselves what is right or wrong. Whatever we decide is automatically correct. We wrongly claim that our decision is the dictate of our "conscience" rather than merely an expression of desire or whim. If I *feel* that it is OK to live with my boyfriend, then I should do so, and my decision is therefore correct! If I'm married and I *feel* that it is OK to have an extramarital affair, then I can do so, and my decision is therefore correct! Again, the important thing, from this perspective, is choice with no restrictions except those placed by the individual himself. "But in this way," said John Paul II, "the inescapable claims of truth disappear."[16]

At the same time, John Paul II noted a conflicting tendency to focus so much on factors that can limit freedom that we deny the existence of human freedom altogether.[17] Some people claim that what we do is caused by things beyond our control – physical, mental, or social circumstances. No one has any moral responsibility, and no one can be blamed for anything.

Neither of these approaches provides a satisfying account of human freedom. If we live as though freedom were directionless, we find that the choices we make are totally self-centered and don't make us happy. On the other hand, we instinctively understand that we are responsible for good and bad decisions. We don't mind evading responsibility for the bad decisions we make, but we do mind it when we don't get credit for the good decisions we make.

In Chapter 6, we saw how we know that we do have freedom of will, that we can and do make choices. "Man is rational and therefore like God; he is created with free will and is master over his acts."[18] Thomas Aquinas notes that if we did not have free will, advice, encouragement, and commands would all be useless.[19]

Free to do what is right

But *why* do we have freedom? The *Catechism* puts it clearly: "God created man a rational being, conferring on him the dignity of a person who can initiate and control his own actions. . . . 'so that he might of his own accord seek his Creator and freely attain his full and blessed perfection by cleaving to him.'"[20]

We can see the relation between freedom, the good, and the truth in a lot of ways. If you give me a boat and tell me how to take care of it, I am free to follow the instructions or reject them. I can freely choose not to follow the instructions, but I may end up destroying the boat in the process. In this case, I am making free decisions, but because I have rejected the truth, I will not have the good of using and enjoying the boat. I will no longer be free to use it. Or, suppose I ask you how to get to your house. If you give me true directions and I choose to follow them, I will get to your house. If I choose not to follow your directions, I will be "free," not tied down by the truth, and lost. Freedom must conform to the truth. In other words, conformity to the truth is a necessary precondition for true freedom.

When he was welcomed at the White House, Benedict XVI, quoting John Paul II, reminded President Bush and the people of the United States that "'in a world without truth, freedom loses its foundation' and a democracy without values can lose its very soul. . . . Those prophetic words . . . echo the conviction of President [George] Washington expressed in his Farewell Address, that religion and morality [are] 'indispensable supports' of political prosperity."[21]

Most people understand and accept the relationship between freedom and the truth when it comes to following directions or manufacturer's instructions. But when it comes to moral choices many people reject the truth. They try to decide what is right and wrong for themselves, without reference to the truth as given through God's law.

"In fact human freedom finds its authentic and complete fulfillment precisely in the acceptance of that law. God who alone knows what is good, knows perfectly what is good for man, and by virtue of his very love, proposes this good to man in the commandments. God's law does not reduce, much less do away with, human freedom; rather, it protects and promotes that freedom."[22] The Commandments are specific requirements of the natural law. God gave them to us so that we will know how to achieve happiness by living in accord with our nature. And God gave us the Church to interpret the natural law and the Commandments so that we will have no doubt about what we ought to do.

Living for Christ, however, is not simply a matter of following rules. There is more to it than a moral code. In his 2000 address on The New Evangelization, Cardinal Joseph Ratzinger, now Pope Benedict XVI, said, "reducing Christianity to moralism loses sight of the essence of Christ's message: the gift of a new friendship, the gift of communion with Jesus and thereby with God."[23] We must obey the natural law and the Commandments. But we are called to go beyond that. We are, all of us, "called to holiness."[24] "All Christians," said the Second Vatican Council, "are called to the fullness of Christian life and to the perfection of charity."[25] In love of neighbor especially, we are called to imitate the self-giving love of the persons of the Trinity – not just a little bit, and not even a lot, but all the way. As the Catechism put it, quoting Saint Gregory of Nyssa, a fourth-century bishop, "Christian perfection has but one limit, that of having none."[26]

God calls us to holiness and perfection as disciples of Christ because he loves us so much that he wants us to enjoy perfect happiness with him. He gives us the gift of freedom so that we can love him of our own accord. He also gives us the natural law and conscience which helps us to judge and apply the truth to concrete actions. Conscience is the link between freedom and the truth. As discussed in Chapter 15, conscience, when properly formed, indicates exactly how we must act to live in accord with the truth, which is the only way we are going to be happy here and hereafter.

Free to be a gift to others

The natural law, the teaching of the Church, and the voice of conscience all enable us to be truly free. Without their guidance, we sink into a self-centered lifestyle that prevents us from living a generous and happy life. If we really understand freedom and live accordingly, we can be a gift to others and be happy.

We *can* be happy. God gives us our intellect so we can know the good, our will so we can desire the good, and the gift of freedom so we can choose the good. If we use these gifts as we should, we will gain true and lasting happiness.

As we saw at the start of this chapter, the key to being truly free is our acceptance and imitation of Christ. In his address to young people gathered at Saint Joseph's Seminary in New York, Benedict XVI stressed that "freedom" depends on truth and that truth "is a discovery of the One who never fails us; the One whom we can always trust. . . . [T]ruth is a person: Jesus Christ. That is why authentic freedom is not an opting out. It is an opting in; nothing less than letting go of self and allowing oneself to be drawn into Christ's very being for others."[27] At the Mass for the inauguration of his pontificate, Pope Benedict XVI told young people why this is so:

> If we let Christ enter fully into our lives, if we open ourselves totally to him, are we not afraid that he might take something away from us? Are we not perhaps afraid to give up something significant, something unique, something that makes life so beautiful? Do we not then risk ending up diminished and deprived of our freedom? And once again the Pope [John Paul II] said: No! If we let Christ into our lives, we lose nothing, nothing, absolutely nothing of what makes life free, beautiful and great. No! Only in this friendship are the doors of life opened wide. Only in this friendship is the great potential of human existence truly revealed. Only in this friendship do we experience beauty and liberation. And so, today, with great strength and great conviction, on the basis of long personal experience of life, I say to you, dear young people: Do not be afraid of Christ! He takes nothing away, and he gives you everything. When we give ourselves to him, we receive a hundredfold in return. Yes, open, open wide the doors to Christ – and you will find true life. Amen.[28]

Endnotes

1   *Gaudium et Spes*, no. 24.

2   *VS*, no. 21.

3   *VS*, no. 13.

4   *CCC*, no. 1716, quoting *Matthew* 5:3–12.

5   *VS*, no. 16.

6   *CCC*, no. 1726.

7   *CCC*, no. 1717.

8   *VS*, no. 16.

9   *CCC*, no. 1831.

10 *CCC*, no. 1832, citing *Galatians* 5:22–23 (Vulgate).

11 *VS*, no. 20.

12 *Giuliana Pelucchi, A Woman's Life* (Boston: Pauline Books, 2002), 124; see generally, Pietro Molla and Elio Guerriero, *Saint Gianna Molla: Wife, Mother, Doctor* (San Francisco: Ignatius Press, 2004).

13 Pope John Paul II, Homily, May 16, 2004, http://www.vatican.va/holy-Father/john-paul-ii/homilies

14 http://www.gianna.org/Biography/.

15 http://www.vatican.va/gpII/dpci,emts/homily-pro-eligends-pontifice-20050418en.html.

16 *VS*, no. 32. We discussed this development in Chapter 15.

17 See *VS*, no. 33.

18 *CCC*, no. 1730, quoting Saint Irenaeus, *Adv. Haeres.*, 4, 4, 3.

19 *ST* I, Q.83, art. 1.

20 *CCC*, no. 1730, quoting *Gaudium et Spes*, no. 17.

21 Pope Benedict XVI, Address at the White House Welcoming Ceremony, April 16, 2008.

22 *VS*, no. 35.

23 Cardinal Joseph Ratzinger, "The New Evangelization," Dec. 10, 2000.

24 *CCC*, no. 2013.

25 *CCC*, no. 2028, quoting Vatican II, *Lumen Gentium*, no. 40.

26 *CCC*, no. 2028, quoting Saint Gregory of Nyssa, *De Vita Mos.*

27 Pope Benedict XVI, Address to Youth, April 19, 2008.

28 http://www.vatican.va/holy_father/benedict_xvi/homilies/2005/documents/hf_ben-xvi_hom_20050424_inizio-pontificato_en.html.

18. MY FAMILY – IMAGE OF THE TRINITY

John Paul II on the family

The previous chapter showed that I ought to be a gift to others. But where do I take lessons in how to do that? The answer: In the family, where I started.

But what is the family? Pope John Paul II said a few important things about it. The family is "the basic cell of society."[1] The "model of the family is . . . in God himself, in the Trinitarian mystery of his life."[2]

"The family originates in a *covenant*, in which man and woman 'give themselves to each other and accept each other.'"[3] This "communion of the spouses gives rise to the community of the family."[4] The covenant and communion of the spouses, similar to "the union of the divine persons"[5] in the Trinity, unites those spouses and "opens them toward a new life . . . an image and likeness of God – a person."[6]

In short, "the conjugal covenant of marriage . . . opens the spouses to a lasting communion of love and of life, and it is brought to completion . . . with the procreation of children. The communion of the spouses gives rise to the community of the family."[7]

It's easy to see how the family relates to the gift of self discussed in Chapter 17. For one thing, "[t]he indissolubility of marriage flows in the first place from the very essence of . . . the gift of one person to another person. This reciprocal giving of self reveals the spousal nature of love. In their marital consent the bride and groom call each other by name: 'I . . . take you . . as my wife (as my husband) and I promise to be true to you . . . for all the days of my life.'"[8]

John Paul II describes the family as "a community of generations."[9] The Fourth Commandment, "Honor thy father and thy mother," was described by John Paul this way: "To *honor* means to acknowledge! We could put it this way: 'Let yourself be guided by the firm acknowledgment of the person, first of all that of your father and mother, and then that of the other members of the family.' Honor is essentially an attitude of unselfishness. It could be said that it is 'a sincere gift of person to person,' and in that sense honor converges with love."[10]

A school of giving

The family is a school in which all the members ought to learn to be a gift of self. What are the natural reasons why the gift of self begins in the family? Each of us is born to a mother and a father. As children we learned to give of ourselves to others in our family. We learned about sacrifice and responsibility as we watched others, especially our father and mother,  making sacrifices and taking on responsibilities for our own well-being. We made sacrifices for others in the family, as a child, and will continue to do so as an adult. As adults, many of us will take on the responsibility of beginning new families. But we first learned about being a gift to others in the family in which we grew up.

These lessons are also important for society. "A family policy," said John Paul II, "must be the basis and the driving force of all social policies."[11] As "the basic cell of society,"[12] the family is where each person is nurtured and educated. Through the family we enjoy the goods of life and love, as parents lovingly accept the gift of each new life and all the members of the family achieve "the good of being together."[13]

Communion of persons

Like the Blessed Trinity, the family is a community of persons united in love. But the family is unlike other communities, unlike a town or a class in school, for example. The family is a community that is founded on communion and complementarity. No living being on earth except man was created "in the image and likeness of God." Human fatherhood and motherhood, while biologically similar to that of other living beings in nature, contain in a unique way a likeness to God which is the basis of the family as a community of human life, as a community of persons united in love.

In the family, the husband and wife give themselves to each other so that they become one flesh. The communion of persons in marriage is so powerful and so complete that the husband and wife are able to cooperate with God in giving new life. From the original loving union of the parents, a new community founded on love arises.

Complementarity

Pope John Paul II noted that the unique communion of persons in the family is possible because of the complementarity of husband and wife. What does this mean and how does it affect the family? Complementarity means that men and women are different, physically and psychologically, but they are equal, and made for each other. Men's and women's bodies are different sexually. Men have the potential to become fathers and women have the potential to become mothers. There are other physical differences that make men physically suited for fatherhood and women physically suited for motherhood. Biological differences are important because they enable us to relate to others as male or female through our bodies. I am called as an adult to relate to others through my body as a man or as a woman, and ultimately, if I marry, as a father or a mother. Another way of saying this is that each of us is called to spiritual motherhood or fatherhood.

The differences between men and women reflect, and arise from, the fact that men and women are made for each other. Sexually, men and women are capable of coming together physically to procreate new persons. Psychologically, men and women complement each other. The qualities that a man or a woman brings to a marriage enrich his or her spouse. A man is not capable of being a wife and a mother, nor is a woman capable of being a husband and a father. "But both are responsible," in the words of John Paul, "for their . . . fatherhood and motherhood. . . . The man and the woman must assume together, before themselves and before others, the responsibility for the new life which they have brought into existence."[14]

What about women's rights?

Men and women are different. But that does not mean that they are not equal. Each person, man or woman, is equal in dignity because each is made in the image and likeness of God. Male and female characteristics complement each other. Neither man nor woman can be reduced to one quality or one function. On May 31, 2004, Cardinal Joseph Ratzinger (now Pope Benedict XVI) issued, with the approval of Pope John Paul II, a letter from the Congregation for the Doctrine of the Faith, entitled, *On the Collaboration of Men and Women in the Church and in the World*. The letter notes, "Although motherhood is a key element of women's identity, this does not mean that women should be considered from the sole perspective of physical procreation. . . . [W]omen should be present in the world of work and in the organization of society and should have access to positions of responsibility which allow them to inspire the policies of nations and to promote innovative solutions to economic and social problems."[15]

This entitlement of women, however, cannot be at the cost of the family, or in a way that destroys the unity of men and women by creating hostility between them. A job that gets in the way of the relationship between mother and child or husband and wife harms everyone, including the woman herself. The letter emphasized this point:

> [A] just valuing of the work of women within the family is required. In this way, women who freely desire will be able to devote the totality of their time to the work of the household without being stigmatized by society or penalized financially, while those who wish also to engage in other work may be able to do so with an appropriate work-schedule, and not have to choose between relinquishing their family life or enduring continual stress, with negative consequences for one's own equilibrium and the harmony of the family. As John Paul II has written, "it will redound to the credit of society to make it possible for a mother – without inhibiting her freedom, without psychological or practical discrimination and without penalizing her as compared with other women – to devote herself to taking care of her children and educating them in accordance with their needs, which vary with age."[16]

Women should not be forced to work outside the home. That is why the Church has long advocated tax or other policies that would provide, in effect, for a "family wage," so that, as Pope John Paul II put it, "[a] workman's wages should be sufficient to enable him to support himself, his wife and his children."[17]

Doesn't the Bible say that wives have to obey their husbands? How does that square with the dignity of women?

In his epistle to the *Ephesians*, Saint Paul states, "Wives, be subject to your husbands, as to the Lord, for the husband is the head of the wife."[18] Some have used this passage to claim that women are inferior to men. Others use it to claim that the Bible is bound by cultural limitations, and, therefore, we can ignore it. Pope John Paul II rejected both of these misinterpretations of *Ephesians*.[19] He points out that this is part of a longer passage in which husbands are exhorted to love their wives with the same kind of sacrificial love that Christ has for the Church. When Saint Paul exhorts husbands to love their wives so much that they are willing to die for them, he affirms the dignity and personhood of women.

Husband and wife are called to a "mutual subjection out of reverence for Christ."[20] "[T]he husband is called the 'head' of the wife as Christ is the head of the Church; he is so in order to 'give himself up for her'. . . . and [that] means giving up even his own life. . . . [I]n the relationship between Christ and the Church the subjection is only on the part of the Church. [I]n the relationship between husband and wife the 'subjection' is not one-sided but mutual."[21] What does this mean? It means that both husband and wife must put aside their own selfishness and sincerely seek to love God and each other, putting their husband's or wife's needs before their own. Original sin causes domination within a marriage; grace helps a husband and wife to overcome this. The virtue of charity enables a husband and wife to order their marriage to Christ. Requiring women to blindly obey the commands of their husbands would be an offense against their freedom and dignity. Exhorting husbands and wives to love each other and order their marriage to Christ affirms the dignity of both. When the question of who's in charge comes up in a marriage, the answer should be "Christ is!"

But aren't there other non-traditional kinds of families?

Many couples today "live together" before they get married. For others, cohabitation, or living together, is an arrangement of self-indulgence and convenience with no thought of marriage. If unwanted children intrude, they can be legally killed by abortion so as not to inconvenience their cohabiting parents. Or those children, if they are allowed to be born, can be abandoned to relatives or others. Or they can be raised by the mother or father after the cohabitation breaks up. In his *Letter to Families*, John Paul accurately described the children of such "free love" arrangements as "orphans of living parents."[22] Whatever else such arrangements are, they are not marriages, and they are not families.

The family is based on the indissoluble covenant between one man and one woman that is ordered to the well-being of the spouses and the procreation and upbringing of children. Only such a union can be recognized and ratified as a "marriage" in society. Only a union between a man and a woman can provide the permanent communion and complementarity that are essential to the well-being of the family and of society. There are many broken families in our society today that are missing the mother, the father, or both. In these cases, there is still a family, but it is not complete. A homosexual union, on the other hand, can never be a marriage. We will discuss this issue in Chapter 20.

So what does all this mean for me?

Each of us is a member of a family here on earth. Each may someday have, or maybe already has, a family of his or her own. God calls us to give of ourselves to those closest to us with a generous and sacrificial love. As we give of ourselves to our family, we strengthen everyone around us, serving as a light to the world. As we'll see in the next chapters, when the natural family is rejected, it affects everyone.

Endnotes

1 *LF*, no. 4.
2 *LF*, no. 6.
3 *LF*, no. 7.
4 *Ibid.*

5   *LF*, no. 8.

6   *Ibid.*

7   *LF*, no. 7

8   *LF*, no. 11.

9   *LF*, no. 10.

10 *LF*, no. 15.

11 *EV*, no. 90.

12 *LF*, no. 4.

13 *LF*, no. 15.

14 *LF*, no. 12.

15 Letter, *On the Collaboration of Men and Women in the Church and in the World* (2004), no. 13 (www.vatican.va).

16 *Ibid.*

17 *CA*, no. 8; see Allan C. Carlson, "Hard Times for Breadwinners: The Fall of the Family Wage since World War II," *The Family in America* (May 1991).

18 *Ephesians* 5:22–23.

19 Pope John Paul II, *Mulieris Dignitatem* (On the Dignity and Vocation of Women), nos. 23–27.

20 *Mulieris Dignitatem,* no. 24; see *Ephesians* 5:21.

21 *Mulieris Dignitatem*, no. 24.

22 *LF*, no. 14.

19. SEX – HOW DID IT GET SO MESSED UP?

Sex is a good thing. The Christian view is upbeat. Sex is a gift of God, who created man, male and female, so that in a covenant of love, they could share in the creation of new citizens for the kingdom of heaven. A covenant is more than just an agreement. It involves a total commitment of each to the other. Marriage is founded on a covenant between a man and a woman involving their total communion for life and leading to the community of the family. "The family, as a community of persons, is . . . the first human society."[1]

In the Christian view, sex has a special, even sacred character. "In the conjugal act, husband and wife . . . confirm . . . the mutual gift of self which they have made to each other in the marriage covenant. The . . . total gift of self to the other involves a potential openness to procreation . . . a mutual communion of love and of life."[2]

We've come a long way . . .

The current attitude toward sex is not what it was in our grandmother's time. Or even in our mother's. Many examples prove this.

According to the Census Bureau, the number of unmarried couples living together grew 72 percent between 1990 and 2000, although married couples still account for 90 percent of the almost 60 million "coupled households." The 5.4 million unmarried couples included nearly 600,000 same-sex couples.

The new data, said Stephanie Coontz of the Council on Contemporary Families, "ties in with everything we know about what's happening all around the world – that more and more couples are cohabiting."[3] The legalization of same-sex "marriages" and "civil unions" or domestic partnerships raises a challenge to the traditional family and sexual morality. Since 1973, over 46 million unborn human beings have been legally executed by surgical abortion, not counting the larger and uncountable number killed by abortion pills and other early-abortion techniques. Public schools distribute condoms, as well as lunch, to 13-year-olds. "Female adolescents ages 15 to 19 have the highest incidence of both gonorrhea and chlamydia, and according to the latest [Centers for Disease Control] figures, 48 percent of new S.T.D. (sexually transmitted disease) cases reported in 2000 occurred among 15-to-24-year-olds."[4] About 19 million new cases of S.T.D.s occur in the United States each year. Cases of gonorrhea, which had been declining, rose sharply in 2006 as syphilis and chlamydia continued to rise.[5] A survey, conducted by the National Domestic Violence Hotline, disclosed in 2008 that half of the "tweens," aged 11 to 14, surveyed are or have been in dating relationships, which for about 30 percent includes sexual relations.[6] According to a study by the Centers for Disease Control, 1 in 4 girls aged 14 to 19 has a sexually transmitted disease; among those who admitted engaging in sexual intercourse, the rate was 40 percent.[7] These and similar statistics reflect a massive cultural shift away from a Christian concept of sex and the dignity of the person. "[P]ornography is a bigger business than professional football, basketball and baseball combined. People pay more for pornography in America in a year than they do on movie tickets [and] all the performing arts combined."[8]

The reason? Contraception.

The purpose of this chapter is not to recite further details but to ask the question: Why has this happened? The answer is simple. The devaluation of marriage and sex is a result of the contraceptive culture which itself results from the alienation of our culture from God. That alienation is a product of the philosophical movement called the Enlightenment. For the past three centuries, philosophers and politicians have applied the errors of the Enlightenment in trying to organize society without God. Those errors are:

Secularism: God does not exist or, if he does, we can't know anything about him and he doesn't care what we do. But as we saw in Chapters 5 and 6. It is unreasonable *not* to believe in God and *not* to believe that God is personal.

Relativism: Nothing is certain. This is absurd because the relativist is certain that nothing is certain. Or if he is not sure that anything is certain, he is certain at least that he is not sure about it.

Individualism: Each individual is his own judge of what is right or wrong for him. He is, in effect, his own god. But an "individualistic concept of freedom," said John Paul II, "ends up by becoming the freedom of 'the strong' against the weak who have no choice but to submit."[9] Moreover, the individualist cannot avoid one limit to his autonomy and control. He can never put himself out of existentice. Whether he agrees or not, his soul will live forever and will be reunited with his body for an eternity of reward or punishment.

As these errors gained public acceptance they were inevitably applied to the most basic human activity, the generation of new life.

"Contraception," wrote Fr. John Hardon, S.J., "goes back to the earliest days of recorded history . . . to as early as 2800 BC."[10] Contraception is the prevention of life while abortion is the taking of life after it has begun. Until 1930, all Christian religions held that contraception was objectively evil. "The father of the Reformation, Martin Luther, lamented, 'How great, therefore, the wickedness of human nature is! How many girls there are who prevent conception and kill and expel tender fetuses, although procreation is the work of God!'"[11]

The Anglican Lambeth Conference of 1930 issued the first declaration by any Christian denomination that contraception could ever be justified under any circumstances. Pope Pius XI denounced Lambeth and restated the traditional Christian position in his 1931 encyclical letter, *Casti Connubii*: "[T]hose who in exercising [the conjugal act] deliberately frustrate its natural power and purpose sin against nature and commit a deed which is shameful and intrinsically vicious. . . . [A]ny use whatsoever of matrimony exercised in such a way that the act is deliberately frustrated in its natural power to generate life is an offense against the law of God and of nature, and those who indulge in such are branded with the guilt of a grave sin."[12]

For the next three decades after Lambeth, contraception grew in popularity but its technology was primitive. With the advent of the contraceptive pill in the 1960s, however, the contraceptive mentality sealed its domination of modern culture.

Is the Church out of step?

Catholics use contraception, including the permanent form of sterilization, at rates comparable to the non-Catholic population of the United States.[13] Yet the Catholic Church continues to teach the traditional Christian rejection of contraception. Is the Catholic Church out-of-step? Shouldn't it bring its teaching into line with the modern world? The answer: No. Contraception is the defining moral issue of our time. And only the Catholic Church has the answer the modern world needs. The Catholic Church offers the way to the Culture of Life. Contraception is the gateway to the Culture of Death. Contraception violates the natural law as well as explicit Church teaching. It is wrong for three reasons:

1. *Contraception is the deliberate separation of the unitive and procreative aspects of sex.* "The two dimensions of conjugal union, the unitive and the procreative, cannot be artificially separated without damaging the deepest truth of the conjugal act itself."[14] For a clear explanation of why this is so, see the

Pastoral Letter of Archbishop Chaput, quoted later in this chapter.

2. *Contraception asserts that man (of both sexes), rather than God, is the arbiter of whether and when life shall begin.* "At the origin of every human person there is a creative act of God. . . . [T]he procreative capacity, inscribed in human sexuality, is . . . a cooperation with God's creative power. . . . [M]en and women are not the arbiters of this . . . capacity, called as they are . . . to be participants in God's creative decision. When, therefore, through contraception, married couples remove from the exercise of their conjugal sexuality its potential procreative capacity, they claim a power which belongs solely to God: the power to decide, in *a final analysis,* the coming into existence of a human person. They assume the qualification not of being cooperators in God's creative power, but the ultimate depositaries of the source of human life. . . . [C]ontraception is . . . so profoundly unlawful as never to be, for any reason, justified. To think or to say the contrary is equal to maintaining that in human life situations may arise – in which it is lawful not to recognize God as God."[15]

3. *Contraception prevents the total mutual self-donation which ought to characterize the conjugal act.* "When couples, by . . . contraception, separate these two meanings that God the Creator has inscribed in the being of man and woman and in . . . their sexual communion," wrote John Paul II, "they act as 'arbiters' of the divine plan and they 'manipulate' and degrade human sexuality and with it themselves and their married partner by altering its value of 'total' self-giving. Thus the innate language that expresses the total reciprocal self-giving of husband and wife is overlaid through contraception, by an objectively contradictory language, namely that of not giving oneself totally to the other. This leads not only to a positive refusal to be open to life but also to a falsification of the inner truth of conjugal love, which is called upon to give itself in personal totality."[16]

What about NFP?

Is natural family planning (NFP) just another type of contraception? The answer: No. In NFP, abstinence is practiced during the period of the month when the woman is fertile and relations are had during the infertile period. During the fertile period, the abstaining couple does nothing. Abstaining would be wrong only if there were a duty to have sexual relations during a given time, but there is no such duty. The parties are merely refraining, by mutual consent and for a serious reason, from the exercise of an act which they are privileged, but not absolutely obliged, to perform. During the infertile period, they do have sexual relations. And they do so in the way that nature dictates, accepting the intrinsic relation between sex and babies. They may have a desire not to have a child at that time, but they are willing to accept whatever happens in the natural performance of the act, and they do nothing to change the act so as to prevent that child.

Now, consider the contracepting couple. They perform the act when they want to perform it, but they take preventive measures to prevent that act from resulting in a new life. If those measures fail and a child is conceived, they may be willing to accept that child rather than kill him (or her) by abortion. But in their contraceptive act they put themselves in charge. In effect, they tell God to get lost. They say to God, "We want to use this privilege, this gift you give us, but we want only part of it. We want the recreational. You keep the procreational. And we will do everything we can in the performance of that act to make sure you don't bother us with a new baby." Ironically, while many couples believe that their contraceptive precautions, their drugs and plugs, will enhance the unitive aspect of sex, the reality is that by willfully rendering it barren, they block and destroy even its unitive character.

NFP and contraception involve "two irreconcilable concepts of the human person and of human sexuality. The choice of the natural rhythms involves accepting the cycle of . . . the woman, and thereby accepting dialogue, reciprocal respect, shared responsibility, and self-control. To accept the cycle and to enter into dialogue means to recognize both the spiritual and corporal character of conjugal communion and to live personal love with its requirement of fidelity."[17]

The privilege of spouses to participate in the procreation of new human life, however, is so important that NFP can be used only if "there are serious motives to space out births, which result from the physical or psychological conditions of husband and wife, or from special circumstances."[18] Pope John Paul II, quoting *Humanae Vitae*, the 1968 encyclical of Pope Paul VI, said in 1990 that, "in relationship to physical, economic, psychological and social conditions, responsible parenthood will be able to be expressed 'either by the deliberate and generous decision to raise a large family, or by the decision, made for serious moral reasons and with due respect for the moral law, to avoid for the time being, or even for an indeterminate period, another birth.'"[19] What motives are sufficient will depend on circumstances of the particular married couple. The advice of a spiritual advisor or confessor can be essential here. What is clear is that NFP cannot morally be used as an alternative, danger-free form of contraception. There must be, in John Paul's words, "a basic openness to fatherhood and motherhood." He emphasized that "it is not possible to practice natural methods as a 'licit' variation of the decision to be closed to life, which would be substantially the same as that which inspires the decision to use contraceptives: only if there is a basic openness to fatherhood and motherhood, understood as collaboration with the Creator, does the use of natural means become an integrating part of the responsibility for love and for life."[20] NFP, in other words, is not an alternative contraceptive used to avoid the physical dangers to the woman presented by most contraceptives.

How Contraception Can Wreck a Marriage

The union of husband and wife should be a total, mutual self-donation. But with contraception there is a holding back, a lack of trust in God – and, before long, in each other. For the contraceptive sexual act is intrinsically an exercise in self-gratification, despite the rhetoric of "caring." Contraception reduces the act to an exercise in mutual masturbation. Archbishop Charles J. Chaput, OFM Cap, of Denver, put this issue so clearly in his 1998 Pastoral Letter on *Humanae Vitae* that it is worth an extended quote:

> The Catholic attitude toward sexuality is anything but puritanical. . . . God created the world and fashioned the human person in his own image. Therefore the body is good. [I]t's . . . a source of great humor for me to listen incognito as people simultaneously complain about the alleged "bottled-up sexuality" of Catholic moral doctrine, and the size of many good Catholic families. (From where, one might ask, do they think the babies come?) Catholic marriage – exactly like Jesus himself – is not about scarcity but abundance. It's not about sterility, but rather the fruitfulness which flows from unitive, procreative love. Catholic married love always implies the possibility of new life, and because it does, it drives out loneliness and affirms the future. And because it affirms the future, it becomes a furnace of hope in a world prone to despair. . . . Catholic marriage is attractive because it is true. It's designed for the creatures we are: persons meant for communion. Spouses complete each other. When God joins a woman and man together in marriage, they create with him a new wholeness; a "belonging" which is so real, so concrete, that a new life, a child, is its natural expression and seal. This is what the Church means when she teaches that Catholic married love is by its nature both unitive and procreative – not either/or.
>
> But why can't a married couple simply choose the unitive aspect of marriage and temporarily block or even permanently prevent its procreative nature? The answer is as simple and radical as the Gospel itself. When spouses give themselves honestly and entirely to each

other, as the nature of married love implies and even demands, that must include their whole selves – and the most intimate, powerful part of each person is his fertility. Contraception not only denies this fertility and attacks procreation; in doing so, it necessarily damages unity as well. It is the equivalent of spouses saying: "I'll give you all I am – except my fertility; I'll accept all you are – except your fertility." This withholding of self inevitably works to isolate and divide the spouses, and unravel the holy friendship between them. . . maybe not immediately and overtly, but deeply, and in the long run often fatally for the marriage.

This is why the Church is not against "artificial" contraception. She is against all contraception. The notion of "artificial" has nothing to do with the issue. In fact, it tends to confuse discussion by implying that the debate is about a mechanical intrusion into the body's organic system. It is not. The Church has no problem with science appropriately intervening to heal or enhance bodily health. Rather, the Church teaches that all contraception is morally wrong; and not only wrong, but seriously wrong. The covenant which husband and wife enter at marriage requires that all intercourse remain open to the transmission of new life. This is what becoming "one flesh" implies: complete self-giving, without reservation or exception, just as Christ withheld nothing of himself from his Bride, the Church, by dying for her on the cross. Any intentional interference with the procreative nature of intercourse necessarily involves spouses' withholding themselves from each other and from God, who is their partner in sacramental love. In effect, they steal something infinitely precious – themselves – from each other and from their Creator.

And this is why natural family planning (NFP) differs

not merely in style but in moral substance from contraception as a means of regulating family size. NFP is not contraception. Rather, it is a method of fertility awareness and appreciation. It is an entirely different approach to regulating birth. NFP does nothing to attack fertility, withhold the gift of oneself from one's spouse, or block the procreative nature of intercourse.[21]

The traditional Christian rejection of contraception makes sense in terms of the human person as created in the image and likeness of God, and in terms of the family as an image of the Trinity "of the communion of the Father and the Son in the Holy Spirit."[22] Like the Trinity, the family is founded on total self-gift.

Is contraception really that bad?

Consider this: The only creating that God has done since the original creation is the creation of each human soul. When we put a male and female dog together, the material forces operate and we get a litter of puppies. But a spiritual soul cannot derive from material elements in that way. "The Church teaches that every spiritual soul is created immediately by God."[23] The spiritual soul of each human being is the result of a separate act of the will of God. And because there is no time in eternity, the creation of that soul was willed by God from all eternity. But God has given to human beings the wondrous power to procreate. That means that he has chosen to depend on human cooperation for the creation of new citizens for the kingdom of heaven. But the contracepting couple throws this invitation back in his face.

What the contracepting couple says to God is something like this: "Look God, for all we know it may be your will that from this act of ours a new human person will come into existence who will live forever. For all we know, that may be your will. *And we won't let you do it.*" Perhaps this may help us understand John Paul II's statement, quoted earlier in this chapter, "[C]ontraception is . . . so profoundly unlawful as never to be, for any reason, justified. To think or to say the contrary is equal to maintaining that in human life situations may arise in which it is lawful not to recognize God as God."[24]

Endnotes

1   *LF*, no. 7.

2   *LF*, no. 12.

3   *Washington Times* (March 13, 2003): A3.

4   Benoit Denizet-Lewis, "Friends, Friends with Benefits and the Benefits of the Local Mall.," *New York Times Magazine* (May 30, 2004): 30, 56.

5   *N.Y. Times*, Nov. 14, 2007, p. A17.

6   *Washington Times*, Feb. 15, 2008, p. A3.

7   *N.Y. Times*, March 12, 2008, p. A1; *South Bend Tribune*, March 12, 2008, p. A1.

8   Frank Rich, "Naked Capitalists," *New York Times* (May 20, 2001), Sec. 6, p. 51.

9   *EV*, no. 19.

10 John A. Hardon, S.J., *The Catholic Family in the Modern World* (St. Paul, Minn.: Leaflet Missal Co., 1991), 1.

11 Sam and Bethany Torode, *Open Embrace* (Grand Rapids, Mich.: Eerdmans, 2002), 62–63; see Allan Carlson, "The Ironic Protestant Reversal: How the Original Family Movement Swallowed the Pill," *Family Policy*, Volume 12, Number 5 (September/October 1999): 16–21.

12 Pope Pius XI, *Casti Connubii*, nos. 54, 56.

13 See Richard Fehring and Andrea Matovina Schlidt, "Trends in Contraceptive Use among Catholics in the United States: 1988–1995," 68 *Linacre Quarterly* (May, 2001): 170; Paul Likoudis, "Government Study Says Contraceptive Use Nearly Universal," *The Wanderer*, Jan. 13, 2005, p. 1.

14 Pope John Paul II, *LF*, no. 12.

15 Pope John Paul II, *Discourse*, Sept. 12, 1983; 28 *The Pope Speaks* (1983): 356, 356–57.

16 Pope John Paul II, *Familiaris Consortio*, no. 32.

17 *Ibid.*

18 Pope Paul VI, *Humanae Vitae*, no. 16.

19 Pope John Paul II, *Address*, Conjugal Responsibility for Love and Life (Dec. 1990), no. 4; *Position Paper* 215 (Nov. 1991): 323, 325; quoting *Humanae Vitae,* no. 10.

20 *Ibid.*, 326.

21 *Catholic World Report* (Oct. 1998): 56, 58–60 (Emphasis added).

22 *CCC*, no. 2205.

23 *CCC*, no. 366.

24 Pope John Paul II, *Discourse* (Sept. 17, 1983): 28. *The Pope Speaks* (1983): 356, 356–57.

20. THE "GREAT DISRUPTION" TRUTH AND CONSEQUENCES

Why is contraception such a big deal?

I don't have to be Catholic to see the cultural impact of contraception. Political scientist Francis Fukuyama said the introduction of the contraceptive pill broke the link between sex and marriage and caused what he called "the Great Disruption" in relations between men and women.[1] "The main impact of the Pill and the sexual revolution that followed," wrote Fukuyama, "was . . . to alter . . . calculations about the risks of sex and thereby to change *male* behavior. The reason that the rates of birth control use, abortions, and illegitimacy all went up . . . is that . . . the number of shotgun marriages . . . declined substantially. . . . Since the Pill and abortion permitted women for the first time to have sex without worrying about the consequences, men felt liberated from norms requiring them to look after the women whom they had gotten pregnant."[2]

"[T]he introduction of widespread contraception use in the 1960s," wrote anthropologist Lionel Tiger, "caused [a] revolutionary break between men and women. It put biological disputes at the center of our national life . . . and placed into question existing moral and religious systems that focused on controlling sexual behavior."[3]

Opposition to contraception is not limited to the Catholic Church. "In the Onan account in Gen. 38:6–10, the Lord demonstrates His vast displeasure with contraceptive behavior. Onan practices withdrawal, and God slays him because he has done an abominable thing. For twenty centuries, Christians recognized this as a teaching against contraception. In Tradition, we read in the first-century Didache a condemnation of contraception. In 1989 Charles Provan wrote *The Bible and Birth Control*, in which he showed that Luther, Calvin, Wesley and about 100 prominent Protestant theologians over the years interpreted the Onan account as a condemnation of contraceptive behavior. Luther called it a form of sodomy; Calvin called it a form of homicide."[4]

Many Protestant-dominated legislatures in the United States, in the nineteenth century, forbade the distribution of contraceptives because they saw contraception as a social evil destructive of the family. The experience of the past four decades validates their judgment. And serious Protestant voices are now raised in support of the traditional Christian rejection of contraception.[5] "Ten years ago," said Milwaukee Pastor Matt Trewhella, "it was virtually unheard of to meet or hear of a Protestant opposed to birth control. Now it is rather commonplace."[6]

The decisive impact of contraception is not a recent discovery. In 1948, Dean William J. Kenealy, s.j., of Boston College

Law School, testified in favor of the Massachusetts laws restricting the distribution of contraceptives. "If a person can violate [by contraception] the natural integrity of the marital act with moral impunity," said Father Kenealy, "then I challenge anyone to show me the essential immorality of any sexual aberration."[7] In contraception, the unitive and procreative aspects of sex are deliberately separated. Man makes himself (or herself) the judge of whether and when life shall begin. Also, contraception denies the mutual and total self-donation that ought to characterize the act of love between husband and wife.

Consider the consequences.

Abortion, suicide and euthanasia. Professor Ralph B. Potter, a Protestant, observed in 1969:

> When a new habit of mind now attributes new life to "rotten luck" in the practice of contraception rather than to the purposeful will of a merciful God, neglect of the countermeasure of abortion becomes [an] irrational and superstitious retreat from the possibility of exercising control of one's destiny. Denial of accessibility to abortion comes to be seen by many as a violation of civil liberty.[8]

If, through contraception, I claim the right to act as the arbiter of when life begins, I will eventually claim the right to act as the arbiter of when life shall end, through suicide or euthanasia as well as through abortion, which is prenatal euthanasia. Euthanasia is merely postnatal abortion. Like abortion, it is a form of murder. The declining ratio of working-age people to the elderly, which is a result of contraception and abortion, creates economic pressure for euthanasia of the elderly, incurably sick, and others described by the Nazis as "useless eaters."

Another premise of the contraceptive ethic is that there is such a thing as a life not worth living. If the value of the child who might be conceived is outweighed by the inconvenience he or she might cause, the first utilitarian answer is contraception, or the use of natural family planning, without sufficient reason, as a risk-free form of contraception. Before that child can even have a chance to come into existence he must pass his first test, a utilitarian exam as to whether he would be more trouble than he would be worth. And if he does begin his life, he must pass a second exam, to determine whether he should be killed by abortion. Under utilitarian ground rules, where innocent life has only relative rather than absolute value, the elderly infirm, the "vegetative," the mentally retarded, and the handicapped, as well as the inconvenient unborn, are predictable losers. And so is the person who comes to regard his own life as not worth living, with suicide as the logical utilitarian choice.

In tracing the "culture of death" to its roots, Pope John Paul describes abortion and contraception as "fruits of the same tree." "[T]he pro-abortion culture," he said, "is especially strong . . . where the Church's teaching on contraception is rejected. . . . The close connection . . . in mentality, between the practice of contraception and that of abortion is . . . demonstrated . . . by the development of chemical products, intrauterine devices and vaccines which, distributed with the same ease as contraceptives, really act as abortifacients in the very early stages of . . . the life of the new human being."[9] The "morning after pill," marketed as an "emergency contraceptive," operates as an abortifacient and is now available over-the-counter without a prescription.[10] Contraception, as the prevention of life, is different from abortion which is the taking of life. But remember that many, if not most, pills and devices which are marketed as contraceptives are really abortifacients because they kill the new human being by preventing his implantation in the womb.[11] In any event, the acceptance of contraception is a root cause of legalized abortion as well as other evils.

Homosexual activity. The contraceptive society cannot deny legitimacy to homosexual activity without denying itself. If it is entirely man's decision whether sex will have any relation to reproduction, if no one can really know what is right and if God's law is excluded, then the objections to allowing two men or two women to marry each other are reduced to the aesthetic and arbitrary.

Let's stop for a minute and review the teaching of the Church on homosexuality. That teaching has three main components:

1. Homosexual acts are always objectively wrong.[12]

2. The inclination toward such acts, like the inclination to excessive drinking, shoplifting or any other immoral act, is an "objectively disordered" inclination.[13] That inclination, however, is not itself a sin.

3. Persons with a homosexual inclination are entitled to respect and have a right not to be unjustly discriminated against. They have a disorder, in their inclination. But their entitlement to respect is important to remember in a culture which disparages those with physical or psychological disabilities or disorders.

To understand this, we should pay close attention to what the *Catechism* says:

Homosexuality refers to relations between men or between women who experience an exclusive or predominant sexual attraction toward persons of the same sex. It has taken a great variety of forms through the centuries and in different cultures. Its psychological genesis remains largely unexplained. Basing itself on Sacred Scripture, which presents homosexual acts as acts of grave depravity,[12] tradition has always declared that "homosexual acts are intrinsically disordered."[13] They are contrary to the natural law. They close the sexual act to the gift of life. They do not proceed from a genuine affective and sexual complementarity. Under no circumstances can they be approved.

The number of men and women who have deep-seated homosexual tendencies is not negligible. This inclination, which is objectively disordered, constitutes for most of them a trial. They must be accepted with respect, compassion, and sensitivity. Every sign of un-just discrimination in their regard should be avoided. These persons are called to fulfill God's will in their lives and, if they are Christians, to unite to the sacrifice of the Lord's Cross the difficulties they may encounter from their condition.

Homosexual persons are called to chastity. By the virtues of self-mastery that teach them inner freedom, at times by the support of disinterested friendship, by prayer and sacramental grace, they can and should gradually and resolutely approach Christian perfection.[14]

The activist homosexual movement seeks to force the law to confer upon a same-sex union the full legal status and name of "marriage," or to confer on a same-sex "civil union" the "legal incidents" (but not the name of) marriage. The "legal incidents" of marriage are the rights, privileges, and obligations which are conferred exclusively by the law on authentic marriage, which is a union of a man and a woman.

But why not allow homosexual couples to marry? One reason is that in the nature of things, the family is founded, as Aristotle put it, on "a union of male and female, that the race may continue."[15] Marriage, as the union of man and woman, goes back to *Genesis* and Adam and Eve.

The law gives exclusive recognition to the man-woman union as marriage because it carries the future and common good of society and of the state. The "common good" is "the sum total of social conditions which allow people, either as groups or as individuals, to reach their fulfillment more fully and more easily."[16] The man-woman union can produce new citizens and, inevitably, new taxpayers. Despite exceptional cases to the contrary, that union is generally ordered to the procreation of *new persons*, to whose education and upbringing the spouses legally and socially commit themselves.

Same-sex couples can make no such commitment. It would therefore be unjust to give such couples the legal status or rights belonging to marriage. "Homosexual unions are . . . lacking in the biological and anthropological elements . . . which would be the basis, on the level of reason, for granting them legal recognition. Such unions are not able to contribute in a proper way to the procreation and survival of the human race. The possibility of using recently discovered methods of artificial reproduction . . . does nothing to alter this inadequacy."[17]

This conclusion of reason is confirmed by the law of God. Through marriage, men and women are given the privilege of living in full and permanent communion and of sharing in the procreation of new persons. Authentic conjugal love is open to new life. Homosexual acts are a dead end with no future. They are intrinsically wrong and the inclination to them, while not sinful, is disordered just as would be an inclination to any other objectively immoral act. Their immorality is compounded by the fact that they are contrary to nature.

Aquinas insisted that the law should not attempt to enforce every virtue or forbid every vice, lest the law be ineffectual and "despised."[18] A law criminalizing private homosexual conduct could invite governmental monitoring of authentic and innocent private activity. It could encourage intrusions that would be harmful to the common good. But it does not follow that a homosexual union should be given the legal status or legal incidents of marriage. The homosexual relationship, in practice as well as in theory, tends to be a parody of authentic marriage.

A study of homosexual men under age 30 in Amsterdam, sponsored by the Dutch AIDS project and published in *AIDS 2003*, found that single men acquire 22 casual partners a year, men with a steady partner acquire 8 casual partners a year, and "steady partnerships" last an average of 18 months.[19] When the European Parliament in 1994 approved same-sex marriage and the adoption of children by homosexual couples, John Paul II said that action "does not merely defend people with homosexual *tendencies* by rejecting unjust discrimination. . . . The Church . . . approves [that]. . . . What is not morally acceptable is the legal approval of homosexual *activity*. . . . [T]he attempt has been made to tell the inhabitants of this continent that moral evil, deviation, a kind of slavery, is the way to liberation, thus destroying the true meaning of the family. The relationship of two men or two women cannot constitute a true family, still less can one grant such a union the right to adopt children. . . . These children suffer . . . grave harm, because . . . they do not have a father and mother, but two fathers or two mothers."[20]

A society in which it makes no legal or social difference whether boys grow up to marry girls or other boys is certifiably insane and is on the road to extinction. Referring to "the strong pressures from the European Parliament to recognize homosexual unions as an alternative type of family, with the right to adopt children," Pope John Paul II, in his last book, Memory and Identity, said, "it is legitimate and even necessary to ask whether this is not the work of another ideology of evil, more subtle and hidden, perhaps, intent upon exploiting human rights themselves against man and against the family.[21] And Benedict XVI described "pseudo-marriages between people of the same sex" as "an expression of anarchic freedom. . . . This pseudo-freedom is based on a trivialization of the body, which inevitably entails the trivialization of the person."[22]

Pornography and the lowering of the dignity of women (and children). In pornography, the woman is treated, not as a person, but as a sex object. In *Humanae Vitae*, Pope Paul VI warned that the acceptance of contraception would cause women to be viewed as sex objects, that "man, growing used to the employment of anti-conceptive practices, may finally lose respect for the woman and, no longer caring for her physical and psychological equilibrium, may come to the point of considering her as a mere instrument of selfish enjoyment, and no longer as his respected and beloved companion."[23] The truth of this prediction can be validated any night of the week on prime-time television. The pornography industry has moved beyond women to focus on child pornography, with children of various ages treated as sex objects.[24]

Extra-marital sex and divorce. In the natural order of things, one reason why sex is reserved for marriage, and why marriage is permanent, is that sex has something to do with babies. The natural law dictates that children be raised by their parents who remain permanently married to each other in a family based on a marriage characterized by fidelity. But if I have the right to decide whether sex will have anything to do with babies, why should I be obliged to reserve sex for marriage? And why should marriage be permanent? Deprived of significance by the severance of its intrinsic relation to new life, sex is trivialized. The sexual act becomes, not a mutual self-donation between covenanted spouses, but an exercise in self-gratification devoid of commitment.

Cloning. The Catholic Church condemns human cloning, the asexual reproduction of a human being who is genetically identical to another person. Cloning shares the premises of contraception. The 1987 *Instruction on Bioethics* said that "attempts . . . for obtaining a human being without any connection with sexuality through . . . cloning . . . are . . . contrary to the moral law, since they are in opposition to the dignity both of human procreation and of the conjugal union."[25] Cloning shares with contraception and IVF (in-vitro fertilization) the treatment of woman as an object of utility, an impersonal egg bank. In "reproductive cloning," the cloned human being is implanted into a woman's womb to be carried to term and born. In "therapeutic cloning," the cloned human being is killed to harvest his stem cells for research or experimentation in the hope that those embryonic stem cells will cure some diseases. "Therapeutic cloning" always involves a homicide of the growing human being. So does embryonic stem cell research (ESCR). Both types of cloning and ESCR are morally wrong as well as socially dangerous. In fact, ESCR, unlike the well-established and moral research on non-embryonic stem cells obtained from the placenta or other tissues, has not succeeded in obtaining a cure of anything.[26] It is futile, however, to try to put the brakes on human cloning or ESCR, as on abortion or euthanasia, without restoring the conviction that God, and not man, is the arbiter of when and how life begins and ends. This requires a reassessment and rejection of contraception.

This book is not the place for a detailed discussion of cloning and related issues. It may be helpful, however, to reflect on the comment of Cardinal Joseph Ratzinger, now Pope Benedict XVI, in his extensive interview with Peter Seewald, published in 2002:

> When we see now how people, with genetic codes available to them, are really starting to pick from the tree of life and make themselves lords of life and death, to reassemble life, then precisely what man was supposed to be protected from is now actually happening: he is crossing the final boundary.
>
> With this kind of manipulation, man makes other men his own artifacts. Man no longer originates in the mystery of love, by means of the process of conception and birth, which remains in the end mysterious, but is produced industrially, like any other product. He is made by other men. He is robbed thereby of his proper status and of his true splendor as a created being.
>
> We do not know all that may happen in this realm in the future, but we can still be certain of this: God will take action to counter an ultimate crime, an ultimate act of self-destruction, on the part of man. He will take action against the attempt to demean mankind by the production of slave-beings. There are indeed final boundaries we cannot cross without turning into agents of the destruction of creation itself, without going far beyond the original sin and the first Fall and all its negative consequences.[27]

Endnotes

1 Francis Fukuyama, *The Great Disruption* (New York: The Free Press, 1999), 101–3, 120–22.

2 *Ibid.,* 102; see also Francis Fukuyama, "At Last, Japan Gets the Pill. Is This Good News?" *Washington. Times* (June 9, 1999): A31.

3 Lionel Tiger, "Nasty Turns in Family Life," *U.S. News & World Report* (July 1, 1996): 57.

4 John F. Kippley, "Truth or Consequences," Lay Witness, June 1996, p. 8, 26.

5 See Charles Provan, *The Bible and Birth Contro,* (Monogahela, Penna.: Zimmer Printing, 1989).

6 Elizabeth Altham, "Converging Paths," *Sursum Corda* (Summer 1998): 60, 61.

7 William J. Kenealy, s.j., "The Birth Control Issue in Massachusetts," 46 *Catholic Mind* (1948): 11.

8 See Kenneth Whitehead, *Respectable Killing: The New Abortion Imperative* (Catholics United for the Faith, 1972), 212.

9 *EV,* no. 13.

10 Charles E. Rice, "Implications of Plan B availability," *The Observer* (Notre Dame), Oct. 31, 2006, p. 8.

11 See, *New York Times* (Mar. 18, 2005): A11; *New York Times* (Dec. 17, 2003): A1.

12 Cf. *Genesis* 19:1–29; *Romans* 1:24–27; *1 Corinthians* 6:10; *1 Timothy* 1:10.

13 Quoting Congregatio n for the Doctrine of the Faith, *Persona Humana,* no. 8.

14 *CCC,* nos. 2357–2359.

15 Aristotle, *Politics,* Book I (Benjamin Jowett, transl.), in *Basic Works of Aristotle* (Richard McKeon, ed., 1941), 1127.

16 *CCC,* no. 1906, quoting *Gaudium et Spes,* no. 1; citing *Gaudium et Spes,* no. 74.

17 Congregation for the Doctrine of the Faith, *Considerations Regarding Proposals to Give Legal Recognition to Unions between Homosexual Persons* (June 3, 2003), no. 7. (Issued by order of Pope John Paul II.)

18 *ST*, I, II, Q. 96, art. 2.

19 *Washington Times* (July 11, 2003): Al.

20 Pope John Paul II, *Meditations* (Feb. 20, 1994): 39 *The Pope Speaks* (1994): 249, 250.

21 Pope John Paul II, *Memory and Identity* (New York: Rizzoli, 2005), 11; *Washington Times* (Feb. 23, 2005): A-13.

22 Pope Benedict XVI, Address, June 6, 2005.

23 Pope Paul VI, *Humanae Vitae* (1968), no. 17.

24 Frank Rich, "Naked Capitalists," *New York Times Magazine* (May 20, 2001): 51; Judith Reisman, "Destructive Effects," *Human Events Online* (Dec. 16, 2003).

25 Congregation for the Doctrine of the Faith, *Instruction on Bioethics* (1987), I, 6; 32 *The Pope Speaks* 137, 146 (1987).

26 *Life Insight* (U.S. Conference of Catholic Bishops) (Nov./Dec. 2004): 1.

27 Cardinal Joseph Ratzinger, *God and the World* (San Francisco: Ignatius, 2002), 134–35.

21. SO, DO I HAVE RIGHTS?
WHERE DID I GET THEM?

Ever read the Constitution of the United States? Let's see. Answer this: Which amendment of the Bill of Rights gives me the freedom of speech and the freedom of religion? If I say, "the First Amendment," it's because I've probably read, or heard something about, the Constitution. But that answer is wrong.

The Constitution does not *give* freedom of speech and of religion to anyone. It *protects* those rights which we already have. Where did we get those rights? As the Declaration of Independence put it, "We hold these Truths to be self-evident, that all Men are created equal, that they are endowed by their Creator with certain unalienable Rights, that among these are Life, Liberty, and the Pursuit of Happiness." In previous chapters we have discussed freedom in the context of our nature as persons created in the image and likeness of God. The Declaration relates to that discussion of moral principles, including the duty to give of ourselves to others, as those principles affect the organization of society and government.

But what are rights?

Prof. Iredell Jenkins, in his important analysis of the nature of rights, identified "two broad views which have disputed the field for centuries:

One of these holds that rights have a real metaphysical and moral status. They are extra- and supra-legal. Rights derive directly from God or Nature – from the ultimate structure of things – and they belong to man as part of his intrinsic nature, as much as do his body, his mind, and his various powers. Law merely recognizes these rights and enforces respect for them. . . .

The other view holds that rights are strictly legal entities or notions. They owe their being and their nature exclusively to law . . . whose creatures they are. Law literally creates rights: the legislative or judicial act accords certain privileges and protections to some persons, and imposes corresponding duties on other persons, and it is this act that brings the right into being and constitutes its content.[1]

The second view described by Professor Jenkins is that of legal positivism, the theory that we have only those rights that the law chooses to give us. The legal positivist would say that, since no one can really *know* what is just or unjust, a law cannot be criticized as being unjust. Therefore every law enacted by the prescribed procedures is valid regardless of its content. As Hans Kelsen, the leading legal-positivist philosopher of the 20th century, put it, "justice is an irrational ideal." Kelsen had the honesty to admit that, under legal-positivist theory, the Nazi regime of death camps and extermination of Jews and other minorities was valid law.[2]

Nazi law defined Jews as nonpersons who were therefore not entitled to any legal rights, including the right to live. In 1857, the Supreme Court of the United States, in the *Dred Scott* case, ruled that freed slaves and their descendants could not be citizens and said that slaves were property rather than persons.[3] Similarly, in *Roe v. Wade*, the 1973 abortion ruling, the Supreme Court held that unborn human beings are nonpersons and therefore have no rights. The Court made unborn children subject to execution at the discretion of others.[4] Think about it. If the youngest human being, in the womb, can be defined as a non-person and deprived of rights, so can his grandmother. And so can I. "A community," said Pope Benedict XVI, "that is built without respect for the authentic dignity of the human being, without remembering that every person is created in the image of God, ends by doing no one any good."[5] If our rights come from the state, or from the people, then the state or the people can redefine or cancel those rights. And I will have no basis for complaint that the cancellation of my rights is unjust.

Where do rights come from?

John Paul II insists, instead, that the "foundation on which all human rights rest" is not the state but "the dignity of the person."[6] That dignity flows from man's creation with an immortal destiny. Every state that has ever existed or ever will exist, has already gone out of business or will do so someday. But every human being who has ever existed, or who ever will exist, will live forever. "[T]he root of modern totalitarianism," said John Paul II in *Veritatis Splendor*, "is in the denial of the transcendent dignity of the human person who, as the visible image of the invisible God, is therefore by his very nature the subject of rights which no one may violate – no individual, group, class, nation or state."[7] In his address to the United Nations, Pope Benedict XVI reaffirmed the reality that "respect for human rights is principally rooted in unchanging justice…. Human rights, then, must be respected as an expression of justice, and not merely because they are enforceable through the will of the legislators."[8]

The higher law

In *Brown v. Board of Education*,[9] the Supreme Court ruled that racially segregated public schools are unconstitutional. Even if publicly enforced racial segregation were constitutional, however, it would still be unjust. That raises two questions: *Why* is legalized segregation, or any other evil, morally wrong and unjust? And *how do I know that?* The answers are in the natural law, discussed in Chapter 14. In his address to the 1986 International Congress on Moral Theology, Pope John Paul II said:

> That there in fact exists a moral good and evil not reducible to other human goods and evils is the necessary and immediate consequence of the *truth of creation*, which is the ultimate foundation of the *very dignity* of the human person. . . . [M]an bears a law written in his heart that he does not give to himself, but which expresses the immutable demands of his personal *being* created by God . . . and . . . endowed with a dignity that is infinitely superior to that of things.[10]

The unjust law

The natural law is the standard for the civil law as well as for personal conduct. When Rosa Parks refused to obey the law requiring her to give up her seat to a white man on the bus in Montgomery, Alabama, in 1955, she made a natural-law statement.[11] A law can be unjust, said Aquinas, "when burdens are imposed unequally on the community."[12] Legally enforced racial segregation, whether on a bus or in a school, is unjust because it violates the dignity of the person and undermines community by its arbitrarily differential treatment of persons.

As Aquinas put it, if a human law "deflects from the law of nature," it is unjust and "is no longer a law but a perversion of law."[13] In his *Letter from Birmingham Jail,* Martin Luther King, Jr. said, "An unjust law is a code that is out of harmony with the moral law."[14] We may be obliged to obey an unjust law, as Aquinas said, to avoid a greater evil of "scandal or disturbance."[15] The Internal Revenue Code contains inequities and even unjust provisions. And the federal government sometimes uses some tax revenues for unjust or immoral purposes, including, for example, its funding of contraception and, in some cases, abortion. But the citizen still has a moral obligation to pay his income tax, to accept his share of the burden of the legitimate things the government does. However, a law that is unjust because it would compel one to violate the divine law must never be obeyed.[16] If a law compelled doctors to perform abortions, a doctor ordered to do so would be obliged to die rather than obey.

. . . and the society that tolerates it

In Chapter 16 we saw how personal sin can become social sin as part of the moral fabric of a society. In the story of Rosa Parks, unjust racial discrimination had become accepted in the culture and required by the law. When Rosa Parks refused to obey the law requiring her to give her seat to a white man, she challenged not only that law but also those "structures of sin" embedded in the culture. Ending such discrimination is not a matter of changing one law, but of changing hearts and minds. This is true not only of racial discrimination, but of any other injustice tolerated or protected by the law, such as abortion and embryonic stem cell research, euthanasia of the elderly and disabled, "prostitution and trafficking in women and children," and "degrading conditions of work which treat laborers as mere instruments of profit." John Paul II described these and other "intrinsically evil" acts as "a disgrace, and so long as they infect human civilization they contaminate those who inflict them more than those who suffer injustice."[17] Ending such evils requires the conversion of hearts and minds. But it also can require changing laws. The law has the power to teach us what is just or unjust. You have an essential role to play here, whether you work to change an unjust law, protest social injustice, courteously discuss the issues with others or, most important, pray for the conversion of people, one by one, to the truth and to justice.

An ultimate choice

What does it really mean to say I must disobey a law that violates the divine law? Consider Saint Mateo Correa Magallanes, a 20th-century hero of the Faith:

As a parish priest, Father Mateo Correa Magallanes, of Tepechitlan, Mexico, administered First Holy Communion to a youth who years later was to become a martyr, Blessed Miguel Pro. As it happened, Father Correa himself was to die for the faith in the same year as his communicant. In 1927, during the Mexican government's continuing persecution of the Catholic Church, Father Correa was arrested by soldiers as he was bringing Viaticum to an invalid. Immediately the priest consumed the host he was carrying to save it from desecration. After spending several days in custody, Father Correa was asked by a military officer, General Eulogio Ortiz, to hear the confessions of some imprisoned members of an insurgency movement, the *Cristeros*. The devoted priest did not decline this opportunity to administer the sacrament. But afterward, General Ortiz demanded of Father Correa, under pain of death, that he reveal the contents of the confessions. Father Correa refused, answering, "But don't you know, general, that a priest must guard the secret of confession? I am ready to die." He was shot to death on February 6, 1927.[18]

General Ortiz was "the law." But Father Correa stood for a higher law. He stood for Christ. Which one do we admire? General Ortiz? Or Father Correa? Which one would we rather be right now – in eternity?

It all comes down to God. "To sum up everything, then, we can say that the ultimate root of hatred for human life, of all attacks on human life, is the loss of God. Where God disappears, the absolute dignity of human life disappears as well. In light of the revelation concerning the creation of man in the image and likeness of God, the intangible sacredness of the human person has appeared. Only this divine dimension guarantees the full dignity of the human person. In the struggle for life, talking about God is indispensable."[19]

Endnotes

1 Iredell Jenkins, "The Concept of Rights and the Competence of Courts," 18 *American Journal of Jurisprudence* (1973): 1, 2.

2 See discussion in Charles E. Rice, *The Winning Side* (Mishawaka, Ind.: St. Brendan's Institute, 2000), 97–101.

3 *Scott v. Sandford*, 60 U.S. (19 How.) 393, 15 L. Ed. 691, 709, 720 (1857).

4 See Rice, *The Winning Side*, 11–21.

5 *L'Osservatore Romano*, English ed., April 4, 2007, p. 2.

6 *EA*, no. 57.

7 *VS*, no. 99.

8 Pope Benedict XVI, Address to United Nations General Assembly, April 18, 2008.

9 347 U.S. 483 (1954).

10 Pope John Paul II, *Address to International Congress on Moral Theology* (Apr. 10, 1986): 31 *The Pope Speaks* (1986): 175, 177.

11 See Juan Williams, *Eyes on the Prize: America's Civil Rights Years*, 1954–55 (New York: Viking, 1967), 59–89.

12 *ST*, I, II, Q. 96, art. 4.

13 *ST*, I, II, Q. 95, art. 2.

14 Martin Luther King, Jr., "Letter from Birmingham Jail," in *Why We Can't Wait* (New York: Mentor, 1963), 76, 82.

15 *ST*, I, II, Q. 96, art. 4.

16 *Ibid.*; see generally, Rice, *50 Questions on the Natural Law*, 83–90.

17 Pope John Paul II, *VS* no. 80, quoting Vatican II, *Gaudium et Spes*, no. 27.

18 *Magnificat* (Yonkers, N.Y., Feb. 2005): 82.

19 Cardinal Joseph Ratzinger, *Address* to Consistory of College of Cardinals, Apr. 4, 1991, "The Problem of Threats to Human Life," *L'Osservatore Romano* English ed. (Apr. 8, 1991): 2; 36 *The Pope Speaks* (1991) 332, 341.

22. DO I EVER HAVE THE RIGHT TO KILL SOMEBODY? WHAT ABOUT SELF-DEFENSE?

Here's the rule: The only time anyone ever has authority to kill anyone *intentionally* is by authority of the state. This is so because the state derives its authority from God who is the Lord of life. "Thou wouldst have no power at all over me," said Jesus Christ to Pontius Pilate, "were it not given thee from above."[1] The state is not the source of fundamental rights, such as the right to life. But the authority of the state is rooted in the natural law. "Every human community needs an authority to govern it. The foundation of such authority lies in human nature. It is necessary for the unity of the state. Its role is to ensure . . . the common good of the society. . . . The authority required by the moral order derives from God."[2]

Justified intentional killing by authority of the state could occur in the just war (or justified rebellion in which the rebels rightly assume the authority of the state); in justified killing in law enforcement;[3] and in the infliction of the death penalty. These situations are up for discussion in Chapters 25 and 26.

Self-defense: a "double effect"

Apart from those cases involving state authority, no private person ever has the right intentionally to kill anyone.[4] But what about self-defense? If a bad guy – let's call him Able – comes at me with a knife and the only way I can prevent him from killing me is to use my .45 caliber pistol to ventilate his forehead between the eyes, can I do it? *Yes*, provided that my intent was to stop him rather than kill him. If, as he was coming at me with the knife, I thought, "This is my chance, at last, to get Able," and then I shot him, I would be morally guilty even though the criminal law would probably not probe that deeply into my motivation. But, if my intent was to stop him from killing me, my act would be morally justified under the principle of the double effect.

An act can have two effects, one good and one evil. My act of shooting Able had the good effect of saving my life and the evil effect of ending Able's. For such an act to be moral, four requirements must be met.[5] 1. The act must be good; 2. sufficient reason exists for permitting the evil effect; 3. the good effect is not obtained by means of the evil effect; and 4. the evil effect is not intended. My killing of Able would be morally justified if it met all those requirements. Defending myself is a good act; I would be justified in using force that could be lethal because I am not obliged to subordinate my life to that of the aggressor; my life  is saved, not because Able died but because he was stopped; and I intended to stop him, not to kill him. I would have the right to kill Able because he was an aggressor. He himself might have been morally innocent by reason of insanity or other cause, but I would have the right to stop him fatally as long as my intent was only to stop him. I did not save my life by killing him, but by stopping him; in the course of stopping him I unintentionally killed him. The principle of the double effect would not justify intentional killing even to achieve a good end. These principles apply also to my right to defend another person who is being attacked.

We need to remember the principle of the double effect. It is the key to solving some difficult moral issues, as we will see in Chapters 23, 24, and 26.

But why can't people shoot abortionists? Wouldn't that save the unborn children they would have killed?

Paul Hill was executed by the State of Florida on September 3, 2003, for the murders in 1994 of abortionist John Britton and his escort, James Barrett.[6] Hill shot them to death as they drove into the parking lot of an abortuary.[7]

Was Hill's act legally or morally justified? No. In legal terms, a person has a legal right to use reasonable force, including deadly force if necessary, to defend his life or that of another. Courts deny this necessity defense to those who block abortuaries to stop the killing of unborn "nonpersons." When his trial judge refused to allow Hill to raise the necessity defense, Hill offered no further defense.[8] Hill shot Britton in the parking lot. Even if the necessity defense applied, it might not legalize Hill's act since he was not defending the unborn child from actual or sufficiently imminent attack. Britton was not performing an abortion when Hill shot him. Instead, Britton, in effect, was commuting to his job as an abortionist.

The moral right to defend oneself or others is governed by the principle of the double effect. If he had been in the abortuary killing room as Britton was doing an abortion, Hill would have had a moral (but not legal) right, and perhaps a moral duty, to stop him by force, although it is inconceivable that deadly force could have been necessary. Hill's intent would have had to have been to stop Britton rather than to injure or kill him.

In the parking lot, Hill killed Britton, not as he was killing an unborn child, but to prevent him from doing so *later*. Hill was not defending the unborn child from an actual or imminent attack. If Hill could morally kill Britton in the parking lot, why could he not kill him in the supermarket? Or in medical school?

Why can't a citizen execute a murderer?

Paul Hill killed Britton because Britton had killed unborn children in the past and, in Hill's judgment, would continue to do so. In killing Britton, Hill essentially made himself judge, jury, and executioner. As a private execution, Hill's act was intrinsically evil. No private person ever has the right intentionally to kill or even to harm anyone. "A man who, without exercising public authority, kills an evildoer," said Saint Thomas Aquinas, is "guilty of murder, and all the more, since he has dared to usurp a power which God has not given him."[9] If an act is "harmful to some other, it cannot be done except by virtue of the judgment of the person" exercising public authority.[10]

In moral terms, the only situations in which anyone ever has the right intentionally to kill anyone are the just war and capital punishment. Both are by authority of the state which derives its authority from God who is the Lord of life. In a justified rebellion, private persons rightly assume the "just war" authority of the state. America is clearly not in a condition of rebellion that could justify Hill's killing of Britton as a combatant in that rebellion. "Armed *resistance* to oppression by political authority is not legitimate, unless all the following conditions are met: 1. there is certain, grave, and prolonged violation of fundamental rights; 2. all other means of redress have been exhausted; 3. such resistance will not provoke worse disorders; 4. there is well-founded hope of success; and 5. it is impossible reasonably to foresee any better solution."[11]

Paul Hill wanted to save unborn children. But he did an objectively evil act and sent a false message. In our relativist, individualist culture, we claim for ourselves the power to decide whether, when, and how life will begin and end, as in contraception, abortion, euthanasia by sedation or by withdrawal of food and water, assisted suicide, stem-cell research, cloning, etc. In his private judgment usurping the authority of God, Paul Hill was a child as well as an opponent of that "culture of death."

The use of violence against abortionists and abortuaries obscures the spiritual nature of the problem and it diverts attention from more useful approaches. The most effective on-site activity in defense of unborn children is prayer and counseling. That activity saves lives, and it can be carried on day after day. The peaceful praying of the Rosary is a powerful weapon at abortuaries, with an appeal beyond denominational lines. Chapter 1 tells a story about the college student who, at the last minute, decided against abortion because of the nun whom she had seen praying the Rosary outside the abortuary. We have no idea how many lives that nun has saved by going, day after day, to witness and to pray for all those involved in abortion.

Legalized abortion will be overcome only through a reconversion of the American people to the conviction that the right to life is sacred because each human being is created in the image and likeness of God with an eternal destiny that transcends the state. Help to women in problem pregnancies and political activity are needed. But the most important step toward that reconversion is prayer, especially the Rosary, since Mary is the mother of life. We should pray for Paul Hill, for his victims and for all those involved in the killing of unborn children, including especially their mothers. But the point to remember is that a good end does not justify the use of an evil means.

Endnotes

1 *John* 19:11.
2 *CCC*, nos. 1898–99, citing Leo XIII, *Immortale Dei*; *Diuturnum Illud*; *Romans* 13:1–2; and *1Peter* 2:13–17.
3 *CCC*, nos. 2265, 2266, 2267.
4 *ST* II, II, Q. 64, art. 3.
5 See Hardon, The Catholic Catechism, 337; Rice, 50 Questions on the Natural Law, 355.

6 *New York Times* (Sept. 4, 2003): A12.

7 *New York. Times* (July 30, 1994): 1.

8 *Newsweek* (Sept. 8, 2003): 52.

9 *ST* II, II, Q. 64; art. 3.

10 *Ibid.*

11 *CCC*, no. 2243.

23. WHAT ABOUT ABORTION?

The governing principle of society, as Pope John Paul II has said, is the dignity of the person. On no other issue is the dignity of the person more at stake than on the right to live.

In *Evangelium Vitae*, John Paul delivered three definitive statements on the absolute inviolability of innocent human life:

1. "[T]he direct and voluntary killing of an innocent human being is always gravely immoral."[1]

2. "[D]irect abortion, that is, abortion willed as an end or as a means, always constitutes a grave moral disorder, since it is the deliberate killing of an innocent human being."[2]

3. "[E]uthanasia is a grave violation of the law of God, since it is the deliberate and morally unacceptable killing of a human person."[3]

Abortion

In his homily at Yankee Stadium, Pope Benedict called for "respect for the inalienable dignity and rights of each man, woman and child in our world – including the most defenseless of all human beings, the unborn child in the mother's womb."[4] The Church teaches that "the human being is to be respected and treated as a person from the moment of conception."[5] The civil law must impose "appropriate penal sanctions for every deliberate violation of the child's rights."[6] The law should not legalize abortion in any case. Nor is an intentional abortion ever morally justified in any case.

But what about the hard cases, where abortion is sought to save the life of the mother, where the pregnancy results from rape or incest or where the unborn child is defective?

Life of the mother

The first "hard" case is where abortion is claimed to be necessary to save the life of the mother. Operations are frequently performed to remove the cancerous womb of a pregnant woman, or to relieve an extra-uterine pregnancy where the child is growing in the fallopian tube or elsewhere outside the womb. Such operations can be performed, even under Catholic teaching, where imminently necessary to save the life of the mother, even though they cause the death of the unborn child. Morally, such operations are justified by the principle of the double effect discussed in Chapter 22, since the death of the child is an unintended effect of an independently justified operation. They do not involve the intentional killing of the child for the purpose of achieving another good. Legally, such operations are not regarded as abortions at all. There is no need, therefore, to provide an exception for such cases in a law prohibiting abortion. Apart from cases such as the extra-uterine pregnancy and the cancerous uterus, there appears to be no medical or psychiatric justification for terminating a pregnancy.[7]

Even if there were a case where an abortion, in the eyes of the law, that is, the *intentional* killing of the unborn child, was necessary to save the life of the mother, it should not be allowed. If two people are on a one-man raft in the middle of the ocean, the law does not permit one to throw the other overboard even to save his own life.[8] Otherwise, might would make right. In maternity cases, the duty of the doctor is to use his best efforts to save both his patients, the mother and her child. He should not be given a license to kill intentionally either of them.

"Never and in no case," said Pope Pius XII in 1951, "has the Church taught that the life of the child must be preferred to that of the mother. It is erroneous to put the question with this alternative: either the life of the child or that of the mother. No, neither the life of the mother nor that of the child can be subjected to direct suppression. In the one case as in the other, there can be but one obligation: to make every effort to save the lives of both, of the mother and the child."[9]

Chapter 17 described how the pregnant Saint Gianna Beretta Molla refused to have a hysterectomy, which could save her life but would cause the death of her unborn child. Instead, she had surgery to remove the dangerous tumor growing in her womb. She insisted, then and later at childbirth, that, if it came to a choice, she wanted her unborn baby's life saved even if it meant that she herself would die. She did not intend to die. She wanted both herself and her unborn child to live. What she meant was that if the situation developed so that the doctors could save only one, she wanted that one to be her baby. She did not give the doctors permission to intentionally kill her in order to save the baby. As it turned out, they both survived the operation to remove the tumor, but the mother was so weakened that she died one week after the birth of the child.

The "defective" child

If an exception should not be made where the life of the mother is concerned, it should not be made for any lesser reason. To allow abortion to prevent injury to the mother's mental or physical health (where her life is not in danger) is to allow killing for what ultimately amounts to convenience. And to kill the unborn child because he may be defective is exactly the basis on which the Nazis exterminated millions of Jews, Poles, Gypsies, and others whose lives they regarded as not worth living.

As discussed in Chapter 9, the Nazi child and adult euthanasia programs, which evolved into the Holocaust, began when the family of a blind, mentally deficient baby, who was missing a leg and part of his arm, asked Adolf Hitler for permission to end their child's life. Hitler not only approved the killing of Baby

Knauer, but used this case as precedent to end the lives of other infants, and of adults, who were disabled and whose lives he deemed not worth living. In deciding that a baby with birth defects should not be allowed to be born, parents who seek an abortion are making themselves the arbiters of which lives are worth living, just as the family of the Knauer infant did. The Church teaches that we may never do anything to intentionally hasten the death of another human being. Some argue, in some cases, that the baby is going to die soon after birth anyway, and the abortion will save the parents from emotional difficulties. But knowing that they have hastened the child's death will only increase the parents' grief. On the other hand, parents who nurtured their dying child to the natural end of his life can attest that the short time they had together was a blessing. These parents will always have the memories of their love for their child unclouded by any guilt over the baby's death. In any event, what is wrong is wrong, always.

Rape and incest

Politically, the most appealing cases to legalize abortion are cases where the pregnancy results from rape and incest. Rape is the broader category. Every act of intercourse by a minor, below the age of legal consent, is rape, whether forcible or statutory or both. The fact that the intercourse is incestuous does not change its character as rape. Pro-abortion literature misleadingly refers to "rape or incest" as if they were totally separate categories. But the only case of pregnancy resulting from incestuous intercourse which would not fall within the broader category of rape would be that resulting from voluntary intercourse with a close relative by an adult woman capable of consent. A victim of rape has the right to resist her attacker. But the unborn child is an innocent non-aggressor and should not be killed because of the crime of his father. Since the woman has the right to resist the rapist, she has the right to resist his sperm. As provided in the United States bishops' Catholic health-care directives, non-abortive measures can be taken, consistent with the law and Catholic teaching, promptly after the rape, which are not intended to abort and which may prevent conception.: "A female who has been raped should be able to defend herself against a potential conception from the sexual assault. If, after appropriate testing, there is no evidence that conception has occurred already, she may be treated with medications that would prevent ovulation, sperm capacitation, or fertilization."[10] However, once the innocent third party is conceived, he should not be killed.

In all cases of troubled pregnancy, the community and, in some cases, the state, has the duty to solve the problems constructively with personal and financial support through birth and beyond. It is not enough merely to forbid the abortion without providing all necessary help. A license to kill, however, is never a constructive solution to a troubled pregnancy.

In abortion, wrote John Paul in *Evangelium Vitae*, "[T]he one eliminated is a human being at the very beginning of life. No one more absolutely innocent could be imagined. In no way could this human being ever be considered an aggressor, much less an unjust aggressor! . . . The unborn child is totally entrusted to the protection and care of the woman carrying him or her in the womb. . . . [T]he decision to have an abortion is often tragic and painful for the mother. . . . Sometimes it is feared that the child to be born would live in such conditions that it would be better if the birth did not take place. Nevertheless, these reasons and others like them, however serious and tragic, can never justify the deliberate killing of an innocent human being."[11]

The principle here is that "civil law. . .can never presume to legitimize . . . an offense against other persons caused by the disregard of so fundamental a right as the right to life. . . . Consequently, a civil law authorizing abortion or euthanasia ceases by that very fact to be a true, morally binding civil law."[12]

Endnotes

1 *EV*, no. 57.

2 *EV*, no. 62.

3   *EV*, no. 65.

4   Pope Benedict XVI, Homily at Mass in Yankee Stadium, April 20, 2008.

5   *EV,* no. 60.

6   Congregation for the Doctrine of the Faith, *Instruction on Bioethics* (1987), III; see Rice, *50 Questions on the Natural Law*, 372–82.

7   See Rice, *The Winning Side*, 221–23.

8   See *Regina v. Dudley and Stephens*, 14 Q.B.D. 273, 15 Cox C.C. 273 (1884); *U.S. v. Holmes*, Fed. Cas. No. 15, 383 (1842).

9   Pope Pius XII, *Address to the Association of Large Families* (Nov. 26, 1951); 53 *AAS* (1951), 855.

10 U.S. Conference of Catholic Bishops, *Ethical and Religious Directives for Catholic Health Care Services* (2001), Directive 36; see discussion in William B. Smith, "Emergency Contraception," *Homiletic and PastoralReview* (March 2004): 68.

11 *EV*, no. 58.

12 *EV*, nos. 71–72.

24. DO WE HAVE TO KEEP GRANDMA ON A FEEDING TUBE FOREVER?

My family can expect to face this problem sooner or later: Grandma is in the hospital, incurably ill. She is comatose or in a persistent vegetative state (PVS). A patient is described as in a "vegetative state" when he is conscious but unresponsive. The British Royal College of Physicians defined it as a "clinical condition of unawareness of self and environment in which the patient breathes spontaneously, has a stable circulation and shows cycles of eye closure and eye opening which may simulate sleep and waking."[1] Grandma receives nutrition and hydration through a tube. She is not dying and not in pain. If food and water are continued, she will live for years. Can we turn off that tube and let Grandma go "home" in peace? Tough question. Fortunately, Pope John Paul II has given us a clear answer.

The basic principles

"[T]he direct and voluntary killing of an innocent human being is always gravely immoral."[2] This includes euthanasia:

> [A]n act or omission which, of itself or by intention, causes death in order to eliminate suffering constitutes a murder gravely contrary to the dignity of the human person and to the respect due to the living God, his Creator.[3]

Each of us also has a moral duty to use all ordinary and proportionate means to preserve our own lives and the lives of those in our care. The civil law permits, but does not require, some acts or omissions forbidden by the moral law. If a patient is competent he can legally refuse all medical treatment, which, in the eyes of the law, includes food and water. If a patient is incompetent, the law permits withholding of treatment, including food and water, based on the patient's previously expressed intent, or based on the decision of his legally recognized health care agent that the patient would have wanted such withdrawal or, in some states, that it would be in his best interest.[4] In moral terms, as declared by Pope John Paul II, that can be euthanasia, as noted below.

An advance directive, which the patient had executed when he was competent, can specify the care to be given to him, and it can designate a person as his health-care agent to make treatment decisions for him. In moral terms, as the U.S. Bishops put it, that decision-maker "may not deliberately cause a patient's death or refuse . . . ordinary means, even if he or she believes the patient would have made such a decision."[5]

Pain killers and other forms of palliative care can morally be given with the intent to relieve the patient's suffering. Even if this results in the unintended shortening of the patient's life, it can be justified under the principle of the double effect.[6]

What about food and water?

As Pope John Paul II has clearly stated, "the administration of water and food, even . . . by artificial means, always represents a natural means of preserving life, not a medical act. Its use [is] ordinary and proportionate, and . . . morally obligatory insofar as and until it is seen to have attained its proper finality, which . . . consists in providing nourishment to the patient and alleviation of his suffering. . . . . [W]aning hopes for recovery . . . cannot ethically justify the . . . interruption of minimal care . . . including nutrition and hydration. Death . . . is . . . the only possible outcome as a result of their withdrawal. . . . [I]t ends up becoming, if done knowingly and willingly, true and proper euthanasia by omission."[7]

The suffering that nutrition and hydration are intended to alleviate is suffering from hunger and thirst, not the suffering from the cancer or other ailment of the patient. Grandma's feeding tube is not supposed to cure her illness but only to sustain her biological life. The fact that it prolongs what some might regard as a pointless existence does not justify its removal. Morally, her feeding tube may be withheld or withdrawn only in three general situations:

1. If it is useless in sustaining bodily life because her body is unable to absorb the nutrients;

2. In the final dying process, when inevitable death is imminent despite the provision of feeding and medical treatments, and the removal of the tube would therefore not be a cause of her death; or

3. If the administration of the nutrition and hydration itself causes unreasonably burdensome pain and suffering to the patient. If the tube were excessively painful, which it rarely is, you could remove it, pursuant to the principle of the double effect, if your intent were to relieve the pain and to replace it if and when it could be done without such pain. If your intent in removing it were to cause Grandma's death for her own good, that removal would be euthanasia, a form of murder.

Euthanasia: legalized on the quiet

We have to view Grandma's predicament in the context of the evolution of American law toward the recognition of suicide and even homicide as a personal right and toward the allowance of the covert practice of euthanasia of some types of patients. In *Roe v. Wade*,[8] the Supreme Court ruled that the unborn child is not a "person" and therefore is not entitled to the constitutional right to life. The Court declined to decide whether the unborn child is a human being. The Court ruled that, whether or not he is a human being, he is a nonperson. The ruling, in effect, is the same as would be a ruling that an acknowledged human being is a nonperson. If the unborn child can be so defined as a nonperson so can members of other target classes. The application of this depersonalization principle is demonstrably moving beyond *Roe v. Wade*. In *Roe*, the Court canceled prohibitions of abortion because the Court wrongly said the unborn child is not a person whose life is protected by the Fourteenth Amendment against deprivation by the state. The courts do not themselves order abortions. The mother makes that decision.

The highly publicized case of Terri Schiavo, who died on March 31, 2005, from court-ordered starvation and dehydration, confirmed the vulnerability of disabled, incompetent persons to legal- ized execution at the decision of others. The Schiavo case has been abundantly analyzed elsewhere.[9] The main purpose of this chapter is to present the basic elements of Church teaching on end-of-life deci- sions. We can note only some aspects of the *Schiavo* case that relate to that subject.

In the *Schiavo* case,[10] Judge George W. Greer of Pinellas County, Florida, Circuit Court, ordered the starvation and dehydration of an innocent, disabled woman who was not dying and was not in significant pain. Judge Greer ordered her execution without affording her the protections mandated for a defendant accused of capital mur- der or even of shoplifting. Judge Greer found that Terri was in a persistent vegetative state (PVS), in the face of contrary evi- dence, and he found, also in the face of conflicting evidence, that she would have wanted her feeding tube removed. He relied on the testimony of her estranged husband, Michael, despite Michael's own conflicting statements and despite his financial and personal conflict of interest that should have caused his removal as guardian. The Florida courts deferred robotically to Greer's findings which they never would have done in a criminal death penalty case. Nor would a convicted murderer's desire to die be considered by any court as a justification for sentencing him to death. But Terri was starved and dehydrated to death because Judge Greer decided she would have wanted that. The federal courts refused Terri the stay of execution which is automatic whenever a condemned murderer brings his case from the state courts to a federal court. In his final order, Judge Greer did not merely authorize Michael to remove Terri's feeding. Nor did he merely order Michael to remove the tube. Rather, Judge Greer, on February 25, 2005, ordered that "the guardian, Michael Schiavo, shall cause the removal of nutrition and hydration from the ward, Theresa Schiavo, at 1:00 p.m. on Friday, March 18, 2005."[11] Even if Terri were able to take nourishment by mouth, as her parents asserted she could, Judge Greer's order would have mandated her execution by starvation and dehydration.[12]

Schiavo is important for reasons beyond judicial abuse. As mentioned at the start of this chapter, food and water may legally be withheld from an incompetent person if there is evidence that he would have wanted that withholding or, in some states, if a court decides that the withholding would be in his best interest. Where the family and caregivers agree that food and water should be withdrawn, it is commonly done without court involvement. The intent to deprive a patient permanently of food and water is essentially an intent to kill. In moral terms it is murder. A benevolent motive does not change that reality. The only reason anyone has heard of the *Schiavo* case is because Michael wanted to kill Terri, and her parents and siblings did not. So the courts got involved. An impasse arising from such disagreement was inevitable in a legal regime which allows family members, who agree, to kill quietly an incompetent relative.

In *Schiavo*, the focus on the persistent vegetative state (PVS), including Governor Bush's petition to intervene on the ground that Terri might not have been PVS, generated an inference that an indisputably PVS patient would want to end his life. *Schiavo* is, in effect, a precedent for courts to order the starvation of PVS patients in reliance on testimony of hostile, court-appointed guardians even against the wishes of family members who want to care for the patient. With diminished public attention, starvation will give way to the painless injection. And the triggering disability will drop below PVS to less serious conditions.

The important point to remember is that the outcome in the *Schiavo* case, which was generally approved by the media, political and academic elites, confirms that we have already crossed the line from state-authorized homicide as in *Roe v. Wade* to state-ordered homicide as in *Schiavo*. The Nazi experience is instructive. When child euthanasia was first authorized, in the *Knauer* case discussed in Chapter 9, it was perhaps not foreseen that, within months the grounds for killing children would include "malformations of all kinds," including "badly modeled ears" and other "defects" including bed-wetting. That program rapidly evolved into adult euthanasia and ultimately the Holocaust.[13]

Are we on the same road as that on which Germany embarked in 1939? Before we answer in the negative, it would be a good idea to reflect on the statement by United States Supreme Court Justice Robert H. Jackson, chief counsel for the prosecution in the trials of Nazi war criminals, in his foreword for the record of the trial involving the Hadamar psychiatric hospital, which the Nazis transformed into an extermination center:

> A freedom-loving people will find in the records of the war crimes trials instruction as to the roads which lead to such a regime and the subtle first steps that must be avoided. Even the Nazis probably would have been surprised themselves, and certainly they would have

shocked many German people, had they proposed as a single step to establish the kind of extermination institution that the evidence shows the Hadamar Hospital became. But the end was not thus reached; it was achieved in easy stages.

To begin with, it involved only the incurably sick, insane and mentally deficient patients of the institution. It was easy to see that they were a substantial burden to society, and life was probably of little comfort to them. It is not difficult to see how, religious scruples apart, a policy of easing such persons out of the world by a completely painless method could appeal to a hardpressed and unsentimental people. But "euthanasia" taught the art of killing and accustomed those who directed and those who administered the death injections to the taking of human life. Once any scruples and inhibitions about killing were overcome and the custom was established, there followed naturally an indifference as to what lives were taken. Perhaps also those who become involved in any killings are not to be in a good position to decline further requests. If one is convinced that a person should be put out of the way because, from no fault of his own, he has ceased to be a social asset, it is not hard to satisfy the conscience that those who are willful enemies of the prevailing social order have no better right to exist. And so Hadamar drifted from a hospital to a human slaughter-house.[14]

The question of Grandma's feeding tube may seem quaint in light of the growing legal sanctioning of the execution of the disabled and others, including, of course, the unborn, whose lives we see as "not worth living." Nevertheless, Grandma's case is very important. The utilitarians would grant her a "merciful release," which in other days was known as homicide. The Catholic Church, virtually alone, says: No!

Grandma's "quality of life" may not be so good. But, as John

Paul said, the value of her life "cannot be made subordinate to any judgment of its quality expressed by other men."[15] No one has a right to decide when Grandma will appear before the judgment seat of God. Nobody has a right intentionally to starve and dehydrate her to death, even if she wanted it and had expressly asked for it. The bottom line? *Feed the hungry. Give drink to the thirsty.*[16]

Endnotes

1 347 *Lancet* (March 23, 1996): 817.

2 *EV*, no. 57.

3 *CCC*, no. 2277.

4 *See Matter of Conroy*, 486 A.2d 1209 (N.J., 1985); Rice, *50 Questions on the Natural Law*, 363.

5 NCCB Committee for Pro-Life Activities, U.S. National Conference of Catholic Bishops, "Nutrition and Hydration: Moral and Pastoral Reflections," p. 7 (April 1992).

6 *EV*, no. 65.

7 John Paul II, *Address* (March 20, 2004), no. 4.

8 410 U.S. 113 (1973).

9 See, for example, O. Carter Snead, "Dynamic Complementarity: Terri's Law and Separation of Powers Principles in the End of Life Context," 57 *Fla. L. Rev.* 53 (2005); Richard J. Stith, "Death by Hunger and Thirst," and Edward J. Furton, "On the Death of Terri Schiavo," 30 *Ethics and Medics* (National Catholic Bioethics Center, June 2005): 1, 3; Michael C. Dorf, "How the Schiavo Federal Court Case Might Have Been Won," *Findlaw's Writ* (March 26, 2005), http://writ.news.findlaw.com/scripts/printer_ friendly.pl?page'/dorf/20050326.html/; Thomas J. Ashcraft, "The Destruction of Terri Schiavo," *The Wanderer* (Apr. 21, 2005): 8; Charles E. Rice, "A State-Ordered Execution," *The Irish Family* (April 15, 2005): 6; Nat Hentoff, "Terri's Tragedy," *Washington Times* (March 28, 2005): A17.

10 For a timeline of the key events in the *Schiavo* case, see Kathy Goodman, "Key Events in the Case of Theresa Marie Schiavo," http://www.miami.edu/ethics/schiavo/timeline.htm/; see, among

the many rulings in the case, *In re Guardianship of Schiavo*, 780 So. 2d 176 (FL App.), cert. denied, 789 So. 2d 348 (FL, 2001); *Bush v. Schiavo*, 885 So. 2d 32 (FL, 2004)

11 *Schiavo v. Schindler* (Pinellas County Circuit Court, File no. 90-2908-GD-003), Order, Feb. 25, 2005, p. 3.

12 See Charles E. Rice, "Schiavo Not to Be Overlooked," *The Observer* (Notre Dame, Ind.; April 7, 2005): 12.

13 See Lifton, *The Nazi Doctors*, 51–52. Fredric Wertham, "The Geranium in the Window: The 'Euthanasia Murders,'" 10 *Child and Family* (1971), 344, 367.

14 *War Crimes Trials,* vol. IV, *The Hadamar Trial,* Earl W. Kintner, ed. (William Hodge & Co., 1949), xiii, xiv.

15 Pope John Paul II, *Address* (March 20, 2004), no. 6.

16 See *CCC*, no. 2447.

25. WHAT ABOUT THE DEATH PENALTY?

OK, intentionally starving Grandma to death would be wrong because she is totally innocent. But what about a serial killer? Or Scott Peterson, who was sentenced to death in California for murdering his wife, Laci, and their unborn child, Conner?[1] Do I have to keep a guy like Scott Peterson alive at state expense? Doesn't he deserve to die?

If the Catholic Church had its way, Peterson would not be executed. *Question:* Why is the Church so protective of murderers, even of one like Peterson?

The "primary aim" of punishment is "redressing the disorder introduced by the offense."[2] This is retribution, restoring the balance of justice. Other purposes are rehabilitation of the offender and deterrence of the offender and of others.

Pope John Paul II, in *Evangelium Vitae* and the *Catechism*, affirmed the traditional teaching that the state, which derives its authority from God, has authority to impose the death penalty to protect the common good. But he has developed the teaching on the *use* of the death-penalty, so that neither retribution nor any other purpose will justify the use of that penalty unless it "is the only possible way of effectively defending human lives against the unjust aggressor. If . . . non-lethal means are sufficient to defend and protect people's safety from the aggressor, authority will limit itself to such means, as these are more in keeping with . . . the common good and . . . the dignity of the human person. Today, . . . as a consequence of the possibilities which the state has for . . . rendering one who has committed an offense incapable of doing harm – without definitively taking away from him the possibility of redeeming himself – the cases in which . . . execution . . . is an absolute necessity 'are very rare, if not practically non-existent.'"[3]

The death penalty, the Church teaches, cannot be justified merely as a means to achieve retribution or to protect society by deterring other offenders. Rather, it must be absolutely necessary to protect other lives from that convicted criminal. Whether execution is such an "absolute necessity" depends on the ability of the prison system to confine that prisoner securely. That involves a prudential judgment. But John Paul's development of the teaching on the use of the death penalty is a universal, not a prudential, criterion. It applies everywhere and to all states.

This severe restriction arises from the importance of the conversion of the criminal. Saint Augustine and Saint Thomas agree that "for a just man to be made from a sinner is greater than to create heaven and earth."[4]

Even under this restrictive teaching of the Church, we could still argue for the death penalty in some cases, for example, if a life inmate, already in maximum security, murders another inmate; or if the state is unable to confine inmates securely. *Evangelium Vitae* and the *Catechism* discuss the death penalty in the context of "preventing crime" and the "system of penal justice." Perhaps this teaching also might not apply to a military tribunal which applies the "laws of war" outside the usual criminal process. In the Revolutionary War, British Major John André, who had conspired with the American traitor, Benedict Arnold, was tried, at General George Washington's order, by military tribunal and hanged as a spy.[5] In 1942, German saboteurs apprehended in the United States were tried by a military tribunal and executed.[6] In a just war, the state has authority to kill intentionally, subject to the restrictions of proportionality and non-combatant immunity. Perhaps, even under John Paul's criteria, execution of a terrorist leader could be justified if his continued imprisonment would incite further terrorist attacks. On the other hand, executing a terrorist leader might make him a martyr in the eyes of his followers, and ultimately might have the same inciting effect. Or, could a terrorist be treated as a spy and rightly executed pursuant to the laws of war? Whatever the answer to such hypothetical cases, John Paul's teaching fully applies to all prosecutions under ordinary criminal law, including that of Scott Peterson.

We cannot dismiss this teaching as merely John Paul's personal opinion – it is contained in the *Catechism of the Catholic Church*, which states: "Assuming that the guilty party's identity and responsibility have been fully determined, the traditional teaching of the Church does not exclude recourse to the death penalty, if this is the only possible way of effectively defending human lives against the unjust aggressor."[7] At the least, it is a teaching of the authentic Magisterium or teaching authority, whether or not the Pope has proclaimed it definitively. As Vatican II declared, "loyal submission of will and intellect must be given, in a special way to the authentic teaching authority of the Roman Pontiff, even when he does not speak *ex cathedra*."[8] As Chapter 13 mentioned, such teachings, even if not proclaimed "with a definitive act," are still binding on all Catholics, requiring us "to take care to avoid those things which do not agree with it."[9]

Cain was a more notorious murderer even than Scott Peterson. Yet God put a mark on Cain, "to protect . . . him from those wishing to kill him. . . . Not even a murderer loses his personal dignity. . . God, who preferred the correction rather than the death of a sinner, did not desire that a homicide be punished by . . . another . . . homicide."[10]

"All together," said John Paul, "We must build a new culture of life. . . . The first . . . step [is] forming consciences with regard to the . . . inviolable worth of every human life."[11]

Some oppose the death penalty because they reject the reality of life after death and, for them, death is therefore the greatest evil. But John Paul has raised the discussion to a new level, based on the immortal destiny of human persons, each of whom is created in the image and likeness of God. "Not even a murderer," he said, "loses his personal dignity."[12] John Paul upheld the dignity of the human person over the claim of the modern state to final dominion over life and death.

This teaching is a serious teaching of the Vicar of Christ. In his challenge to our pagan culture of death, John Paul insists that God – not the individual and not the state – is in charge of the ending as well as the beginning of life. Moreover, our "freedom . . . possesses an inherently relational dimension" because "God entrusts us to one another."[13] Therefore, "every man is his 'brother's keeper.'" Even if my brother, like Cain – or Scott Peterson – is a murderer.

The death penalty is a deceptive quick fix that distracts attention from basic problems. As Archbishop Charles Chaput of Denver said, "Capital punishment is just another drug we take to ease other, much deeper anxieties about the direction of our culture. Executions may take away some of the symptoms for a time (symptoms who have names and their own stories before God), but the underlying illness – today's contempt for human life – remains and grows worse."[14]

The Church's remedy for that "contempt for human life" is to seek the protection of society and of innocent life, not through homicidal acts of the state, but through a "cultural transformation" building a "new culture of life," recognizing "the incomparable and inviolable worth of every human life."[15]

Endnotes

1   *Washington Times* (March 17, 2005): A6.

2   *CCC*, no. 2266.

3   *CCC*, no. 2267, quoting John Paul II, *Evangelium Vitae*, no. 56.

4   *ST* I, II, Q. 113, art. 9.

5   Terence P. Jeffrey, "Military Tribunals: Constitutional, Legal and Just," *Human Events* (Nov. 26, 2001): 3.

6   *New York Times* (Nov. 15, 2001): B6.

7 *CCC*, no. 2267.

8 *Lumen Gentium*, no. 25.

9 Code of Canon Law, no. 752.

10 *EV*, no. 9.

11 *EV*, nos. 95 and 96.

12 *EV*, no. 9.

13 *EV*, no. 19.

14 http://www.originsonline.com (June 26, 1997).

15 *EV*, no. 95.

26. BUT CAN'T I KILL PEOPLE AND BREAK THINGS IN A WAR?

Yes, if the war is a "just" one.

What's a just war?

The "just war" theory is a method of moral reasoning, to prevent war and to minimize its effects if it does occur. The basic requirements for *jus ad bellum*, justice in going to war, as summarized by Saint Thomas, are: proper authority, just cause, and right intention:

> In order for a war to be just, three things are necessary. *First*, the authority of the sovereign by whose command the war is to be waged. For it is not the business of a private individual to declare war, because he can seek for redress of his rights from the tribunal of his superior. Moreover, it is not the business of a private individual to summon together the people, which has to be done in wartime. . . . *Second*, a just cause is required, namely that those who are attacked, should be attacked because they deserve it on account of some fault. . . . *Third*, it is necessary that the belligerents should have a rightful intention, so that they intend the advancement of good, or the avoidance of evil.[1]

The *Catechism* lists further details that must be met before going to war can be justified. "[T]he damage inflicted by the aggressor . . . must be lasting, grave, and certain"; war must be a last resort, with "all other means . . . impractical or ineffective"; "there must be serious prospects of success"; and "the use of arms must not produce evils . . . graver than the evil to be eliminated."[2]

What can I do in a war?

Jus in bello, justice in fighting a war, requires proportionality and discrimination.[3] Proportionality means that tactics and weapons used must not cause excessive incidental civilian damage or casualties in relation to the military situation.[4] Discrimination requires non-combatant immunity from intentional attack. As the Catholic Bishops of the United States said in their 1983 pastoral, the principle of discrimination "prohibits directly intended attacks on noncombatants and nonmilitary targets."[5] In the words of the Second Vatican Council, "every act of war directed to the indiscriminate destruction of whole cities or vast areas with their inhabitants is a crime against God and man, which merits firm and unequivocal condemnation."[6] World War II provided numerous possible examples of such mass bombings of urban areas by both sides in that conflict. The attack on the World Trade Center on September 11, 2001, is certainly another example.[7]

A military response, therefore, cannot legitimately target noncombatants. Pursuant to the principle of the double effect,[8] however, it can be morally justified to attack a military target of sufficient importance even though the attacker knows, but does not intend, that noncombatants will be killed in the attack. The key is the intent. No one ever has the moral right intentionally to kill the innocent. But the good act of attacking the legitimate target may be justified even though it has the unintended evil effect of killing the innocent, provided that the good effect of the attack is not obtained by means of the evil effect and provided there is sufficient reason for permitting the unintended evil effect.

Suppose, in a just war waged, for example, by the United States, an enemy military unit uses a populated area to set up a stronghold from which to inflict heavy casualties and possible defeat on an American unit. That American unit could be justified in targeting that enemy unit even though civilians in that populated area would foreseeably, or inevitably, be killed. The civilians could not be directly and intentionally targeted. However, at some point we would have to conclude that the unintended loss of civilian lives is so disproportionate that the attack itself could not rightly be made. A further consideration, peculiar to nuclear war, is whether the risk of escalation to a war of total destruction is so great as to preclude any use of nuclear weapons. This risk of escalation is present in any conflict but it could be especially acute if large, non-tactical nuclear weapons were used.

Does the government have a blank check on war?

The discussion of just war theory in this chapter is not intended to offer any judgment on the moral legitimacy of any particular war, including the Iraq War commenced in 2003 or any other conflict. Pope John Paul II has emphasized that war "is always a defeat for humanity" and cannot be waged "except as the very last option and in accordance with very strict conditions."[9]

In his message for the World Day of Peace, on January 1, 2002, John Paul said that "Terrorism . . . is itself a true crime against humanity. There exists, therefore, a right to defend oneself against terrorism, a right which . . . must be exercised with respect for moral and legal limits in the choice of ends and means."[10] The Pope, however, strongly expressed his disagreement with the proposed war in Iraq.[11]

In their statement opposing the Iraq War, the United States Catholic Bishops said, "There are no easy answers. Ultimately, our elected leaders are responsible for decisions about national security."[12] Similarly, the *Catechism* notes that the "evaluation" of the conditions for a just war "belongs to the prudential judgment of those who have responsibility for the common good."[13] As the Bishops implicitly acknowledge, the public does not have a right to disclosure of facts where that would be contrary to national security. The governmental decisions here are entitled to the benefit of the doubt.

A preventive war, incidentally, is not intrinsically wrong, although it is more difficult to justify. Cardinal Joseph Ratzinger, before he became Pope Benedict XVI, expressed his own opposition to the Iraq War and observed that "the concept of preventive war does not appear in the *Catechism*. We cannot simply say that the *Catechism* does not justify war, but . . . the *Catechism* has developed a doctrine which . . . does not deny that there are values and populations that must be defended, in certain circumstances, and . . . proposes a very precise doctrine on the limits of these possibilities."[14]

All wars are debatable. As Bishop Wilton Gregory, president of the Conference of Catholic Bishops, said on the Iraq War, "While we have warned of the potential moral dangers of embarking on this war, we have also been clear that there are no easy answers. War has serious consequences; so could the failure to act. People of good will . . . disagree on how to interpret just war teaching and how to apply just war norms to . . . this case. We understand and respect the difficult moral choices that must be made by our president and others."[15] The political authorities, however, are morally bound by the objective moral norms embodied in the just war requirements.

Suppose I object to war?

The teaching of the Church properly limits the right of the state to engage in war. This important teaching, however, lends no support to those who would disparage the men and women who defend the community through the honorable profession of arms. "Those who are sworn to serve their country in the armed forces," says the *Catechism*, "are servants of the security and freedom of nations. If they carry out their duty honorably, they truly contribute to the common good of the nation and the maintenance of peace."[16]

But what if we conscientiously object to participation in war? "Public authorities," the *Catechism* says, "have the right and duty to impose on citizens the *obligations necessary for national defense.*"[17] But the *Catechism* goes on to say that, "Public authorities should make equitable provision for those who for reasons of conscience refuse to bear arms; these are nonetheless obliged to serve the human community in some other way."[18] The law of the United States provides exemption from military service to those who are opposed in conscience to all war but not to those who are opposed merely to the war in question.[19]

What can I really do for peace?

On a positive note, we can do something real for the cause of peace. Our weapons are the Eucharist and the Rosary. "[T]he most effective way of establishing peace on the face of the earth," said John Paul II, "is through . . . Perpetual Adoration of the Blessed Sacrament."[20] "The time you spend with Jesus in the Blessed Sacrament," said Blessed Mother Teresa of Calcutta, "will help bring about an everlasting peace on earth."[21]

Pope John Paul II had proclaimed October 2002–October 2003 as The Year of the Rosary.[22] He went on to proclaim the period from October 2004 to October 2005 as a special Year of the Eucharist.[23] In doing so, he emphasized "the need for a

Eucharistic spirituality" and pointed to "Mary, 'woman of the Eucharist,' as its model."[24]

After he was shot in Saint Peter's Square by an assailant on May 13, 1981, John Paul II attributed his survival to Our Lady of Fatima. Our Lady had appeared to three young children in Fatima, Portugal, on May 13, 1917, and each month thereafter until October 13, 1917. The Pope journeyed to Fatima to offer thanks to Mary for his survival of the attempt on his life. He said in his homily at Fatima, on May 13, 1982, "the message of Our Lady of Fatima is a motherly one, it is also strong and decisive. It sounds like John the Baptist speaking on the banks of the Jordan. It invites to repentance. It gives a warning. It calls to prayer. It recommends the Rosary. . . . [T]he . . . call to repentance and conversion, uttered in the Mother's message, remains ever relevant." With good reason, Mary's message at Fatima has been called "a peace plan from Heaven."[25]

"More than ever," said John Paul II, "our troubled world, which began the new millennium with the specter of terrorism and the tragedy of war, demands that Christians experience the Eucharist as *a great school of peace*, forming men and women who, in social, cultural and political life, can become promoters of dialogue and communion. May we be helped by the Blessed Virgin Mary, whose whole life incarnated the meaning of the Eucharist."[26] Mary and the Eucharist go together as weapons *against* war.

Endnotes

1   *ST* II, II, Q. 40, art. 1 (emphasis added).

2   *CCC*, no. 2309.

3   See *CCC* nos. 2312–14.

4   See the discussion of the Geneva Convention in Gregory G. Gillette, "Proportionality in the Law of War," *Marine Corps Gazette* (Sept. 2003),. 60.

5   U.S. National Conference of Catholic Bishops, "The Challenge of

Peace: God's Promise and Our Response," May 3, 1983, no. 107, p. 34; see also *CCC*, no. 2314.

6   *Gaudium et Spes*, no. 80.

7   See, for example, the analyses of some of the more notable cases in: Andrew Roberts, "Dresden: An Atrocity or a Justifiable Act of War?" *Daily Mail* (London) (Feb. 11, 1995): 8; Raymond H. Willcocks, *The Ethics of Bombing Dresden*, (U.S. Army War College, 1998); Alexander McKee, *Dresden 1945: The Devil's Tinderbox* (Dutton, 1984); Frederick Taylor, *Dresden: Tuesday, February 13, 1945* (Harper Collins, 2004); Nicholas D. Kristof, "The Bomb: An Act That Haunts Japan and America," *New York Times* (Aug. 6, 1995): Sec. 1, p. 1; Eric Talmadge, "Tokyo Remembers Night to Rival Hiroshima," *Washington Times* (March 10, 1993), A16; Peggy Noonan, "Courage Under Fire," *Wall Street Journal* (Oct. 5, 2001): http://www.opinionjournal.com/columnists/pnoonan/archive/.

8   See Chapter 22 of this book.

9   Pope John Paul II, Address to Vatican Diplomatic Corps, Jan. 13, 2003; 32 *Origins* (2003): 543–44.

10   Pope John Paul II, "No Peace Without Justice, No Justice without Forgiveness," 47 *The Pope Speaks* (July/Aug. 2002): 234, 235–36.

11   Pope John Paul II, *Angelus Address* (March 16, 2003); *Zenit News Agency* (March 16, 2003).

12   U.S. Conference of Catholic Bishops, *Statement on Iraq War* (Nov. 13, 2002).

13   *CCC*, no. 2309.

14   Cardinal Joseph Ratzinger, "From September 11 to Iraq," *Avvenire* (Sept. 21, 2002): 25.

15   *Our Sunday Visitor* (April 6, 2003): 17.

16   *CCC*, no. 2310, citing *Gaudium et Spes*, no. 79.

17   *Ibid.*

18   *CCC*, no. 2311, citing *Gaudium et Spes*, no. 79.

19   See discussion in Rice, *The Winning Side*, 295–97.

20   Missionaries of the Blessed Sacrament, *Newsletter*, no. 34 (Sept. 2000).

21   Missionaries of the Blessed Sacrament, *Newsletter*, no. 58 (Sept. 2002).

22 Pope John Paul II, *Homily* (June 10, 2004); 49 *The Pope Speaks* (2004): 345.

23 Pope John Paul II, *Mane Nobiscum Domine* (Oct. 7, 2004), no. 4–10; 50 *The Pope Speaks* (2005): 47, 48–50.

24 Pope John Paul II, *Homily* (May 13, 1982); 27 *The Pope Speaks* (1982): 240, 244, 246.

25 *Our Lady of Fatima's Peace Plan from Heaven* (Rockford, Ill.: TAN Books, 1983).

26 *Mane Nobiscum Domine*, nos. 27, 31.

27. WHY IS THIS A GREAT TIME TO BE HERE?

Don't Be a Dope, Follow the Pope.

This banner greeted Pope John Paul II when he spoke to young people in Sydney, Australia, in 1995.[1] My accent may be different, but the message is still true for me today.

In 1990, Fr. Francis Canavan, S.J., wrote that "Christendom, the society in which Christianity could be taken for granted, has ended. . . . With its final disappearance, we shall . . . see no more . . . nominal or post-Christian Catholics. The gap between Catholicism and the general culture will be so wide . . . that we shall all have to take our stand on one or the other side of it."[2]

Why is this a great time for me to be here? Because the choice is clear: the other side has nothing to offer, and I *am* on the winning side. "A new phase in the history of freedom is opening up," said Pope John Paul II to American Bishops in 1998, "[T]he time is right. For *other culture-forming forces are exhausted . . . or lacking in intellectual resources . . .* to satisfy the human yearning for genuine liberation" even if those forces still . . . exercise a powerful attraction especially through the media."[3]

Only in the social and moral teachings of the Catholic Church will I find a complete answer to the problems of a culture built on the denial of both God and reason. If reason cannot know objective moral truth, all that is left is a conflict of interests with the victory to the strongest or the most unscrupulous.

The pontificate of Pope John Paul II rescued not only Faith but also Reason. His epistemology (a fifty-cent word meaning the science of knowing) is called realist because it affirms that the human mind is really able to connect with, and understand, the world and unchanging morality.

This is a great time to be here because the younger generations coming up are more in tune with objective truth – and with Christ who is Truth with a capital T – than are most of their elders. John Paul promised that "[T]he future of the world and the Church belongs to the *younger generation.*"[4] In his 1979 address to high school students at Madison Square Garden in New York, he said, "We are convinced that only in Christ do we find real love. . . . When you wonder about the mystery of yourself, look to Christ who gives you the meaning of life. When you wonder what it means to be a mature person, look to Christ who is the fullness of humanity. And when you wonder about your role in . . . the world . . . look to Christ. Only in Christ will you fulfill your potential as an American citizen and as a citizen of the world community."[5]

The theme of hope continues beyond Pope John Paul II. Pope Benedict XVI, at the Mass for the Inauguration of his Pontificate, rejected any note of pessimism: "[T]he Church is alive. . . . And the Church is young. She holds within herself the future of the world and therefore shows each of us the way towards the future. The Church is alive and we are seeing it: we are experiencing the joy that the Risen Lord promised his followers. The Church is alive because Christ is alive, because he is truly risen. . . . God, who became a lamb, tells us that the world is saved by the Crucified One, not by those who crucified him. The world is redeemed by the patience of God. It is destroyed by the impatience of man."[6]

Meeting Christ in the Eucharist

If "the world is saved by the Crucified One," wouldn't it make sense for us to spend some time with him? One of the signs of hope in the Church is the resurgence of adoration of Christ in the Blessed Sacrament. In his homily closing the 2000 World Youth Day, attended by 2 million young people in Rome, John Paul urged them: "[W]hen you go back home, set the Eucharist at the center of your personal life and community life. Love the Eucharist, adore the Eucharist and celebrate it, especially on Sundays, the Lord's Day. Live the Eucharist by testifying to God's love for every person."[7] A continuing theme with John Paul II is his belief that "the . . . surest and the most effective way of establishing peace on the face of the earth is through the great power of Perpetual Adoration of the Blessed Sacrament."[8]

Archbishop Fulton J. Sheen, the great preacher of the mid-20th century, made a holy hour of adoration before the Blessed Sacrament every day of his priestly life. He said: "[T]he Holy Hour is not a devotion; it is a sharing in the work of redemption. . . . In the Garden, Our Lord contrasted two 'hours' – one was the evil hour, 'this is your hour' – with which Judas could turn out the lights of the world. In contrast, Our Lord asked: 'Could you not watch one hour with Me?' . . . He asked for an hour of reparation to combat the hour of evil. . . . Not for an hour of activity did He plead, but for an hour of companionship. . . . God is . . . inviting us to come to Him . . . to ask for such things as we need and to experience what a blessing there is in fellowship with Him."[9] When Mother Teresa was asked, "What will convert America and save the world?," she replied: "my answer is prayer. What we need is for every parish to come before Jesus in the Blessed Sacrament in holy hours of prayer."[10]

Is it really the Body and Blood of Christ?

In his *Credo of the People of God*, Pope Paul VI explained this doctrine:

> [T]he Mass . . . is the Sacrifice of Calvary rendered sacramentally present on our altars. We believe that as the bread and wine consecrated by the Lord at the Last

Supper were changed into His Body and His Blood . . . likewise the bread and wine consecrated by the priest are changed into the Body and Blood of Christ. . . . This mysterious change is . . . called by the Church *transubstantiation*. . . . [I]n the reality itself, independently of our mind, the bread and wine have ceased to exist after the Consecration, so that it is the adorable Body and Blood of the Lord Jesus that from then on are really before us under the sacramental species of bread and wine. . . . The . . . existence of the Lord . . . is rendered present by the Sacrament in the many places on earth where Mass is celebrated. And this existence remains present . . . in the Blessed Sacrament which is, in the tabernacle, the living heart of each of our churches.[11]

Transubstantiation

Transubstantiation. Is it *really* true? Yes. The Latin prefix, "trans," means "across." What goes across, or changes, at the consecration is the substance of the bread or wine. The substance of a thing is *what* it is. The substance of chalk is that it is chalk. The appearances (technically called accidents) can vary without changing its nature as chalk. It can be long, short, square, green, powdered, etc. But whatever its accidents or appearances, it is still chalk. At Christ's ascension, as the apostles "were gazing up to heaven as he went, behold, two men stood by them in white garments and said to them, 'Men of Galilee, why do you stand looking up to heaven?'"[12] The "two men" were angels. Their appearance was that of men, but their substance was that of angels.

When the priest pronounces the words of consecration in the Mass, the substance of the host is changed from bread to the Body of Christ and the wine is changed to the Blood of Christ. The appearances remain those of bread and wine, but substantially they are no longer bread and wine.[13] They are truly the Body and Blood of Christ. "Christ is present, whole and entire, in each of the species" of bread and wine. The Eucharist should be at the center of our life, both in the Mass and in our adoration of the Blessed Sacrament.[14]

The Eucharist as Powerhouse

In his apostolic exhortation, Sacrament of Love, Benedict XVI stresses that "adoration outside Mass prolongs and intensifies all that takes place during the [Mass] itself. Indeed, 'only in adoration can a profound and genuine reception mature. . . . [T]his personal encounter with the Lord . . . strengthens the social mission contained in the Eucharist, which seeks to break down not only the walls that separate the Lord and ourselves, but also and especially the walls that separate us from one another.'"[15]

Adoration of the Eucharist, therefore, is not some kind of sterile, self-centered devotion. Rather, it has a social impact. "[T]he sacrifice of Christ is for all," Benedict said, "and . . . the Eucharist thus compels all who believe in him to become 'bread that is broken' for others, and to work for the building of a more just and fraternal world. . . . The Lord Jesus, the bread of eternal life, spurs us to be mindful of the situations of extreme poverty in which a great part of humanity still lives: these are situations for which human beings bear a clear and disquieting responsibility."[16]

One way that Christ inspires us to put our faith into action is the "works of mercy," through which we provide spiritual as well as bodily help to those in need. "Instructing, advising, consoling, comforting are spiritual works of mercy, as are forgiving and bearing wrongs patiently. The corporal works of mercy [include] feeding the hungry, sheltering the homeless, clothing the naked, visiting the sick and imprisoned, and burying the dead. Among all these, giving alms to the poor is one of the chief witnesses to fraternal charity: it is also a work of justice pleasing to God."[17]

Mary, Mother of the Eucharist

Chapter 26 noted that Mary and the Eucharist go together. "When at the visitation she bore in her womb the Word made flesh," said John Paul II, "She became . . . the first 'tabernacle' in history."[18] Mary was the first who turned bread and wine into the Body and Blood of Christ, when she carried and nourished the unborn Christ in her womb. At the marriage feast at Cana, Mary invited us, "Do whatever he tells you."[19] "With the same maternal concern," said John Paul, "Mary seems to say to us: 'Do not waver; trust in the words of my Son.'"[20] In the same spirit, Pope Benedict XVI, in addressing the Cardinals who had elected him Pope, said, "to the Virgin Mother of God, who with her silent presence supported the steps of the nascent Church, and comforted the faith of the apostles, I commend all of us and the expectations, hopes and concerns of the whole community of Christians. Under Mary's maternal protection, Mater Ecclesiae, I invite you to journey in docility and obedience to the voice of her divine Son and our Lord Jesus Christ."[21]

St. Louis de Montfort said, "God has never made and formed but one enmity; but it is an irreconcilable one, which shall endure and grow even to the end. It is between Mary, His worthy Mother, and the devil – between the children and the servants of the Blessed Virgin, and the children and tools of Lucifer. The most terrible of all the enemies which God has set up against the devil is His holy Mother Mary."[22] At Fatima, Our Lady told the three young people to whom she appeared, to "Say the Rosary every day to obtain peace for the world."[23] One of Benedict XVI's first acts as pope was to venerate the image of Our Lady of Guadalupe, which is located at the highest point in the Vatican Gardens. "[W]e again place our lives in your maternal hands. . . . With great hope, we turn to you and trust in you," he prayed.[24]

The free gift of youth

Pope John Paul II reminds me that "conversion consists in commitment to the person of Jesus Christ, with all the theological and moral implications taught by the Magisterium of the Church."[25] At the 10th World Youth Day in Manila John Paul told the young people: "False teachers . . . belonging to an intellectual elite . . . present an anti-Gospel. They declare that every ideal is dead . . . . [T]heir only certainty is that there is no definite truth. . . . They want you to be like them – doubtful and cynical. . . . [T]hey advocate an approach to life that has led millions of young people into a sad loneliness in which they are deprived of reasons for hope and incapable of real love. . . . In *Crossing the Threshold of Hope* I have written that 'the fundamental problem of youth is profoundly personal. Young people . . . know that their life has meaning to the extent that it becomes a free gift for others.'" He concluded with a question and a challenge for every young person; a question and challenge for each of us:

> A question therefore is directed to each one of you personally. Are you capable of giving of yourself, your time, your energies, your talents, for the good of others? Are you capable of love? If you are, the Church and society can expect great things from each one of you.[26]

In his address in New York to young people, Pope Benedict urged them "to consider four essential aspects of the treasure of our faith": personal prayer and silent contemplation, liturgical prayer, charity in action, and vocations. "Nourished by personal prayer, prompted in silence, shaped by the Church's liturgy you will discover the particular vocation God has for you. Embrace it with joy. You are Christ's disciples today. Shine his light upon this great city and beyond. Show the world the reason for the hope that resonates within you. Tell others about the truth that sets you free."[27]

Endnotes

1   *South Bend Tribune* (Jan. 18, 1995): A6.

2   Francis Canavan, s.j., "Commentary," *Catholic Eye* (Feb. 20, 1990), 2.

3   43 *The Pope Speaks* (1998): 238, 241 (emphasis added).

4   Pope John Paul II, *Tertio Millennio Advenienti* (1994), no. 58.

5   Pope John Paul II, "The Church Wants to Give You Jesus Christ,"

24 *The Pope Speaks* (1979), 320, 321; *The Pope in America* (The Wanderer Press, 1979), 28.

6 http://www.vatican.va/holy_Father/Benedict_XVI/homilies/documents/hp_ben_xvi_hom_200.

7 30 *Origins* (Aug. 31, 2000), 184–85.

8 Pope John Paul II, *Ecclesia in Eucharistia*, no. 25.

9 Fulton J. Sheen, *Treasure in Clay* (Garden City, N.Y.: Doubleday, 1980), 188–90.

10 For Eucharistic quotations from Mother Teresa and for further information on Eucharistic Adoration, contact Missionaries of the Blessed Sacrament, P.O. Box 1701, Plattsburgh, NY 12901; (518) 566–7103.

11 Pope Paul VI, *The Credo of the People of God* (1968).

12 *Acts* 1:10–11.

13 *CCC*, no. 1377; *Ecclesia de Eucharistia*, no. 15, quoting Pope Paul VI, *Mysterium Fidei* (1965).

14 See *CCC*, nos. 1377, 1378, 1380.

15 Pope Benedict XVI, Sacramentum Caritatis (Sacrament of Love) (2007), No. 66.

16 *Ibid.*, nos. 88–90.

17 *CCC*, no. 2447, citing *Tobit* 4:5–11; *Sirach* 17:22; *Matthew* 6:2–4; 25:31–46.

18 *Ecclesia de Eucharistia,* no. 55.

19 *Jn.* 2:5.

20 *Ecclesia de Eucharistia*, no. 54.

21 Pope Benedict XVI, Address (April 22, 2005), no. 5.

22 St. Louis de Montfort, *True Devotion to Mary* (The Fathers of the Company of Mary, 1941; reprint ed., Rockford, Ill.: TAN Books, 1985), 30–31.

23 *Our Lady of Fatima's Peace Plan from Heaven* (TAN Books, 1983).

24 *L'Osservatore Romano* (English edition) (May 25, 2005): 2.

25 *EA*, no. 53; see also *EA*, no. 33.

26 40 *The Pope Speaks* (1995), 161, 162. *Washington Times* (Jan. 15, 1995): A7.

27 Pope Benedict XVI, Address to Youth, April 19, 2008.

RECOMMENDED READINGS

The authors encourage readers of this book to continue their study of the issues discussed and especially of the teachings of the Church on those issues. Useful sources include, in addition to the works cited in the notes to this book, the Old and New Testaments, the *Catechism of the Catholic Church*, and the encyclicals and other papal statements, including especially those of Pope John Paul II and Pope Benedict XVI. Papal encyclicals and other statements can be found on the Vatican website, www.vatican.va.

INDEX

Abbreviations, xiii
Abel, 112, 118
Abortion, and contraception, 155–56; as grave evil, 178–82; as social sin, 169; defective child, 180–81; killing of abortionists, 174–76; life of the mother, 179–80; rape and incest, 181–82; *Roe v.* Wade, 55–56; teaching of Church on, 178–82; violence as tactic against, 174–76
Abortionists, killing of, 174–76
Abstraction, 17–18, 21–22
Acts of the Apostles, 49, 73, 80
Ad Gentes, 81, 99
Ad Tuendam Fidem, 88
Adam and Eve, 10, 45–48, 59–64, 77, 89, 158, 162
Adoration of the Eucharist. *See* Eucharistic Adoration.
Alexander, Leo, 100
Altham, Elizabeth, 163
André, John, 194
Andrews, Julie, 3, 28
Angels, creation of and sin of, 44–45, 59–60; role of, 44–45, 50–51
Anglican community, 76, 144
Annunciation, 66

Anointing of the Sick, 80
Apostles, 11, 90
Aquinas, Saint Thomas. *See* Saint Thomas Aquinas.
Aristotle, 163
Arnold, Benedict, 194
Ashcraft, Thomas J., 191
Atonement, 65
Auschwitz, 12, 118
Australia, 206

Baptism, 80, 89
Baptist community, 76
Barrett, James, 174–75
Beatitudes, 124
Belief, universal, as proof of existence of God, 31
Benedictus Deus, 25
Bible and Birth Control, The, 154
Bible, claimed as infallible guide, 86–88; Protestants and, 86–88
Bioethics, Instruction on, 161–62, 178, 183
Blessed Mother. *See* Mary, Mother of God.
Blessed Sacrament, 202–3, 208. *See* Eucharist.
Blessed Sacrament, Missionaries of the, 202, 204, 213
Bloom, Allan, 4, 8

Body, resurrection of, 47–48
Bonaparte, Napoleon, 27
Booker, Frank E., xi
Boston College Law School, 154–55
Britton, John, 174–75
Brown v. Board of Education, 167–68
Bruskewitz, Fabian, 25
Bush, George W., 129
Bush, Jeb, 189
Bush v. Schiavo, 192

Cain, 112, 118, 195
California, 193
Calvin, John, 154
Campbell, Dwight P., 13
Canavan, Francis, 206
Canon Law, 85, 88, 197
Carlson, Allan, 151
Casti Connubii, 144
Catechism of the Catholic Church, angels, 44–48; baptism of desire, 89; Beatitudes, 124; common good, 158, 172; community, human, 58, 158, 172; *Compendium of the Catechism*, 81, 118–19; conscience, 102, 106–7; conscientious objection, 201–3; Church, functions of, 79; Church, marks of, 74–78; Church, mission of, 78–79; Church teaching, as binding, 82–88, 91, 195; Commandments, Ten, 92–98, 104–5, 109; creation, 3, 7, 44–49, 50–57, 150; death penalty, 193–96; euthanasia, 184, 191; God, attributes of, 41–43; happiness, 3–4, 7; grace, 25, 79–80, 89;

homosexuality, 157–58, 163; human and divine knowledge of Christ, 70–71, 73; human reason, 17–18; Hypostatic Union, 67, 72; Jesus Christ, general, 69–73; Judgment, Particular and Last, 24–25, 120–21; justification, 25; love, 42–43; Magisterium, 11–13, 82–88; mercy, works of, 213; man, in image and likeness of God, 46–49, 50–59, 111–12; moral act, the, 98–99; natural law, 95, 96–98; organ transplants, 23–25; Paschal Mystery, 72; Protoevangelium, 65, 72; rebellion, justified, 175; Revelation, 10–11, 13, 90–91; sacraments, 79–80; saints, communion of, 120–21; Scripture and Tradition, 87–88; salvation, 25; sin, 118–20; sin, original, 61–64; Spirit, Holy, 124–25; state, authority of, 172; Trinity, 41–43, 66, 111–12, 150; virtues, 113–17; war, 198–203
Catholic Health Care Services, Ethical and Religious Directives for, 183
Catholics, "cafeteria," 84–88
Census Bureau, 141–42
Centisimus Annus, 8, 58, 140
Chambers, Whittaker, 30, 33
Chaput, Charles, 145, 148–50, 196
Charity, virtue of, 116–18
Chesterton, Gilbert K., 82
Christian communities, 78
Chroust, Anton-Hermann, 99
Church, Catholic, abortion,

178–82; and Holy Spirit, 74, 78; as Mystical Body of Christ, 74, 91, 107; as People of God, 74; bishops of the United States, 191, 200–201, 203–4, 206; Canon Law, 85, 88, 197; conscience, 104–7; conscientious objection, 169, 201–3; death penalty, 193–96; Eucharist, 57, 78, 80, 87, 206–12; euthanasia, 184–91; evangelization, 81; infallibility of, 82–84; liturgy, 212; Magisterium, 11–13, 79, 82–88, 104–5, 195, 211–12; marks of, 74–78; natural law and, 89–101; necessity of, 82–88; Pope as Vicar of Christ, 107, 196; "subsists," church of Christ, in Catholic Church, 77–78; teaching function of, 82–88; unity of, 74–75; war, 198–203

Churches, oriental, 78

Cloning, 161–62

Cohabitation, 138–39, 141–42

Commandment, Fourth, 134

Commandments, Ten, 10, 53, 91–92, 95, 98, 104–5, 109, 129

Commandments, Ten, exceptions to, 96–99

Common good, 99, 158

Communism, 30

Computer, analogy to intellect, 16–18

Concupiscence, 60–64, 94–95

Confession, seal of, 169–70

Confirmation, 80

Congregation for the Doctrine of the Faith, 78, 81, 163–64

Conroy, Matter of, 191

Conscience, 102–9; as proof of existence of God, 30–31, 33, 103; definition and function of, 102–4; duties to, 104–7

Constitution of the United States, 165, 186–87

Contraception, 86–87, 107, 141–51, 153–64

Contradiction. *See* Non-contradiction, principle of.

Coontz, Stephanie, 142

Corinthians, First Letter to the, 42, 57, 72–73, 110, 121, 163

Council of Chalcedon (451), 67

Council of Constantinople II (553), 43, 72

Council of Constantinople III, 73

Council of Contemporary Families, 142

Council of Florence (1439), 25

Council of Lyons II (1274), 25

Council of Orange II (529), 122

Council of Toledo XI (675), 43, 121

Council of Trent (1546–1563), 25, 49, 64, 122

Council, Lateran V (1513), 49, 57

Cowsert, Mary, ix

Creation, 44–49, 50–58

Credo of the People of God, 42–43, 57, 208–9, 213

Cristeros, 170

Crossing the Threshold of Hope, 212

Culpability, 95–101

Culture of death, 54–56, 144, 155–56

Culture of life, 144, 195–96

Daniel, 57

Davitt, Thomas E., 100

Death penalty, 172, 193–96

Death, brain, 23, 25; definition and nature of, 23–25
Death, culture of, 55–56
Decalogue. *See* Commandments, Ten.
Declaration of Independence, 165
Dei Verbum, 13, 88, 100
Denizet-Lewis, Benoit, 151
Denver, 148, 196
Descartes, René, 18–19
Deus Caritas Est, 116–17, 122
Deuteronomy, 100
Didache, 154
Dignity, human, 52–56, 167, 170
Discrimination, racial, 167–69
Diuturnum Illud, 176
Divorce, 161
Dogmatic Constitution on the Catholic Faith. See Lumen Gentium.
Dolan, James H., 25, 36–40
Dominus Iesus, 81
Dorf, Michael C., 191
Double effect, principle of, 172–76, 179–80, 185–86, 199–200
Dred Scott Case, 166
Dresden, 204
Drummey, James J., 64, 68

Ecclesia de Eucharistia, 213
Ecclesia in America, 167
Elliott, Lawrence, 13
Enlightenment, errors of, 142–44
Ephesians, Letter to the, 43, 80, 136–39
Episcopalian community, 76
Epistemology, realist, 207
Essence, 16–18
Eucharist, 57, 78, 80, 87, 202–3, 206–12
Eucharistic Adoration, 202–3, 206–12

European Parliament, 159–60
Euthanasia, 55–56, 155–56, 169, 184–91; advance directives, 185; definition, 184; nutrition and hydration, 185–89
Evangelium Vitae, 8, 58, 101, 121, 140, 151, 161, 163, 178–83, 191, 193–97
Evangelization, 129–30
Evil, definition of, 93
Evolution, 47–49
Ex cathedra, 84, 86
Exodus, 100

Faith and Reason. See Fides et Ratio.
Faith, relation to reason. *See* Reason, relation to faith.
Faith, virtue of, 116
Familiaris Consortio, 151
Families, Letter to, 133–39
Families, non-traditional, 138–39
Family wage, 136–37
Family, the, 133–39
Farnan, Casey, 16–17
Farnan, Elizabeth Anne, v
Farnan, James Bernard, v
Farnan, Jeanne Frances, v
Farnan, Joseph Terence, v
Farnan, Kathleen Mary, v
Farnan, Mary Rose, v
Farnan, Michael Anthony, v
Farnan, Michael, v
Farnan, Paul Daniel, v
Farnan, Sarah Catherine, v
Farnan, Theresa, x–xi
Father, God the, 41–43
Fatima, Our Lady of, 203, 205, 221–23
Fehring, Richard, 151
Fides et Ratio, xi, 7–8, 27–33, 64, 110

First Amendment, 165

Florida, 174–75, 187–89

Food and water. *See* Nutrition and hydration.

Fortitude, virtue of, 114–15

Fourteenth Amendment, 186–87

Fox, Deb, ix

Fox, George, 76

Francis Mary, Brother, 13

Franciscan University of Steubenville, xi

Franciscans, 6

Free will, 37–40, 50–51, 128

Freedom, 123–24, 127–31

Fukayama, Francis, 153, 163

Furton, Edward J., 191

Gabriel, angel, 66

Gagnon, Edouard, 8

Galatians, Letter to the, 64, 132

Gaudium et Spes, 7–8, 49, 57, 58, 80, 99–100, 121, 131–32, 163, 171, 204

Gebhardt, Karl, 91–92

General Motors, 83

Genesis, 41, 43, 48–50, 57, 64, 72, 121, 154, 158, 163

Geneva Convention, 203

Germany, 194, 204. *See also* Nazis.

Gibbons, James, 76–77, 81

Gift of self, 123–34, 150

Gillette, Gregory G., 203

Glenn, Paul, 35–40

God is Love. See Deus Caritas Est.

God, as judge, 24–25, 120; as Truth, 11; attributes of, 34–40; creation by, 3, 41, 44–49, 50–64; existence, 2–3, 5, 7, 26–33; loss of, 4; our knowledge of through reason, 9–10,

26–33, 34–40; Revelation by, 10–11, 41–43; Trinity, 10, 41–44, 59–60, 65–73, 111–12, 135.

Golden Rule, the, 106

Good, definition of, 93

Goodman, Kathy, 191

Gorres, Albert, 103

Grace, actual, 5, 79–80; definition of, 25; habitual, 79–80; sanctifying, 79–80; sufficiency of, 89

Greer, George W., 187–89

Gregory, Wilton, 201

Guadalupe, Our Lady of, 211

Guerriero, Elio, 132

Guilt, feeling of, and conscience, 103–4

Gypsies, 180

Habits, 113

Hadamar hospital, 189–90

Hadamar Trial, The, 192

Hagerty, Cornelius, 18–19

Hail Mary, 99

Hardon, John A., 6, 35, 40, 67–68, 72, 110, 143, 176

Hayes, Edward J., 64, 88

Hayes, Paul J., 64, 88

Heaven, 1–2, 21, 24–25, 44–45, 53–54, 120–21

Hebrews, Letter to the, 80

Hell, 1, 24–25, 120–21

Henry VIII, 76

Hentoff, Nat, 191

Hill, Paul, 174–75

Himmler, Heinrich, 91

Hinckley, John, 95

Hiroshima, 204

Hitler, Adolf, 4, 55, 180–81

Holocaust, 180–81

Holy Hour, 208

Holy Orders, 80
Holy Spirit. *See* Spirit, Holy.
Homosexual activity, 156–60
Homosexual marriage. *See*
    Marriage, same-sex.
Homosexual Persons,
    Considerations Regarding
    Proposals to Give Legal
    Recognition to Unions
    Between, 163
Homosexuality, Church teaching
    on, 156–60
Hope, virtue of, 116, 207
Humanae Vitae, 147–52, 160
Humani Generis, 49, 57
Hypostatic Union, 67–68

Idea, definition of, 18; nature and
    formation of, 16–18
Immortale Dei, 176
Impeccability, 84
In vitro fertilization, 161–62
Incarnation of Jesus Christ, 10,
    65–72
Inclinations of man, 93–95
Individualism, 143
Infallability, 83–84
Inside the Vatican, 81
Intellect, active and passive,
    16–18; acts of, 17
Internal Revenue Code, 168
Iraq War, 200–201, 204
Islam, 2

Jackson, Robert H., 189–90
Japan, 163, 204
Jeffrey, Terence P., 196
Jenkins, Iredell, 165
Jesus Christ, xi, 56; as Truth, 6;
    Ascension, 72, 209; Beati-
    tudes as portrait of, 124;

Eucharist, 57, 78, 80, 87,
    200–3, 206–12; hope for
    future in, 206–12; human
    nature of, 65–73; Hypostatic
    Union, 66–67; Incarnation, 10,
    65–73; knowledge of, 69–73;
    Messiah, 65; Passion, 72;
    Redeemer, 65–73; reparation
    by, 65–66; Resurrection, 72;
    reveals dignity of man, 56;
    second person of Trinity,
    65–73; superabundant
    justification by, 71–72
Jews and Nazis, 4, 180–82
Jews, extermination of. *See* Nazis.
John the Baptist, 203
Judgment by intellect, 17
Judgment, Last, 24–25, 120–21;
    Particular, 24–25, 120–21
Jus ad bellum, 198–99
Jus in bello, 199
Justice, virtue of, 114

Kazakhstan, 2, 7
Keefe, Patricia, 13
Kelsen, Hans, 166
Kenealy, William J., 154–55
Kill, right to, 172–76, 184–85
King, Dwight, ix
King, Martin Luther, 168
Kinslow, Carmela, ix
Kinter, Earl W., 192
Kippley, John F., 163
Knauer, Baby, 55, 180–81, 189
Kolbe, Maximilian. *See* Saint
    Maximilian Kolbe.
Kristof, Nicholas, 204

Lambeth Conference, 144
Lamentabili Sane, 73
Law, divine, 169–70; natural,

53–56, 87, 89–101, 167–69;
natural, exceptions to, 96–98;
unjust, 168–70
Lawler, Ronald, 64
Lawler, Thomas C. 64
Legal positivism. *See* Positivism,
legal.
Letter from Birmingham Jail, 168
*Letter to Families. See Families,
Letter to.*
Lifton, Robert Jay, 58, 192
Likoudis, Paul, 151
Love, definition of, 42–44
Lucifer, 211
Lumen Gentium, 27, 32, 34–39,
49, 80–81, 88, 99, 132, 197
Luther, Martin, 76, 143, 154
Lutheran community, 76

Madison Square Garden, 207
Magnificat, 171
Man, creation of, 44–58; dignity
of, 54–55
Mane Nobiscum Domine, 205
Manicheanism, 53
Manila, 211
Marriage, 133–39, 141–51, 161
Marriage, same-sex, 139, 141–42,
157–60
Martyrs, 11–13
Mary, the Mother of God, 12, 63,
67–68, 121, 202–3;
Assumption of, 12; Eucharist
and, 210–12
Mass, Sacrifice of the, 79, 208–10
Material, distinguished from
spiritual, 20–25
Matrimony, sacrament of, 80
McKee, Alexander, 204
Medical treatment, obligatory,
184–85

Mercy, corporal and spiritual
works of, 191
Methodist Episcopal community,
76
Mexico, 12, 169–70
Military tribunals, imposition of
death penalty by, 194
Mishawaka, Indiana, 1–2
Molla, Gianna Beretta. *See* Saint
Gianna Beretta Molla.
Molla, Gianna Emmauela, 126
Molla, Pietro, 132
Monro, Margaret T., 122
Moral Act, the, elements of,
98–99
Moral Theology, International
Congress on, 168
Morality, objective, 4–5
Morality, statistics, 141–42
Mulieris Dignitatem, 140
Mulligan, James, 99, 100
Murphy, Edward J., xi
Mysterium Fidei, 213

Natural Family Planning, 146–47,
155–56
Natural Law. *See* Law, natural.
Nature, definition of, 42
Navy, United States, 99
Nazis, 4, 12, 55, 91–92, 155, 166,
180–81, 189–90
Necessity, defense of, 175–76
New Testament, 10–11, 87–88,
90–91
New York, 207, 212
Newman, John Henry, 30–31, 33,
103
Non-contradiction, principle of,
15–16, 92
Noonan, Peggy, 204
North Vietnam, 99

Nostra Aetate, 31, 33
Notre Dame Law School, ix, xi
Notre Dame, University of, x–xi, 29
Nuremberg trials, 91–92, 189–90
Nutrition and hydration, 184–91; permissible withholding of, 185–86

Oesterle, John and Jean, 100
Old Testament, 10–11, 90–91
On the Collaboration of Men and Women in the Church and in the World, 136–37, 140
Onan, 154
Ortiz, General Eulogio, 170

Palliative care, 185
Papacy, as gift, 86–88
Parks, Rosa, 169
Paschal, definition of, 72
Patna, 57
Peace, weapons to achieve, 202–3, 207–12
Peace, World Day of, 200
Pelucchi, Giuliana, 132
Penance, sacrament of, 80
Person, definition of, 42; dignity of, 56
Peterson, Conner, 193
Peterson, Laci, 193
Peterson, Scott, 193, 195
Philemon, Letter to, 72–73
Pilate, Pontius, 172
Pill, morning-after, 155–56
Pill, the, 153–64
Plawecki, Lois, ix
Poles, 180
Pontifical Academy of Sciences, 48–49
Pope Benedict XII, 25
Pope Benedict XVI, 86, 107, 121–22; abortion, 178; Church, youth of, 207; conscience, 103–4; creation, 48–49, 54; dialogue, x, xii; dignity of the human person, 167; ecumenism, 78; Eucharist, 210–13; evolution, 48–49; faith and reason, 7; freedom and truth, 129–31; God, need for, 7, 103–31; hope, 117, 207; love, 116–17; Jesus Christ, relation to freedom and truth, 130–31; Mary, 210–12; Paschal Mystery, 72; Purgatory, 121; reason, 6; rights, 167; same-sex "marriage," 160; secularism, 2; United States visit, 2, 7–8, 112, 129–31, 178; women, 136–37; youth, 112, 130–31, 206–13. *See also Cardinal Joseph Ratzinger, Deus Caritas Est* and *Spe Salvi*.
Pope John Paul II, abortion, 156, 178–82; Beatitudes, 124; Cain and Abel, 112; Christ, look to, 207; Church teaching, authoritative, 88; conscience, 109; contraception, 145–47, 150–52, 156; culture, 2, 7, 55–56, 144, 156, 195–96, 206; culture of death, 55, 156; culture of life, 144, 195–96; death and funeral of, 56; death penalty, 86, 193–96; Descartes and Aquinas, 18–19; Eucharist, 202–3; euthanasia, 178, 184–86, 191; evil, intrinsic, 168, 169; evolution, 48–49; faith and reason, xi, 2, 6–7, 27, 206–7; family,

133–36; God, known by
reason, 29, 32–34, 39; God,
need for, 4; homosexuality,
159–60; hope, 210–12; killing
of innocent, 178; Mary,
202–3; person, dignity of the,
56, 167; natural law, 92,
96–97, 168; relativism, 4,
127–28; renaissance of
Christianity, 6; rights, 167;
Rosary, 202–3; terrorism, 200;
totalitarianism, 167; truth,
teaching of, 5–7; shooting of,
65–66, 203; war, 198–203;
women, 136–37; youth, x, xii,
206–12;. *See also Centisimus
Annus*, *Ecclesia in America*,
Evangelium Vitae, *Familiaris
Consortio*, *Fides et Ratio*,
Letter to Families, *Mulieris
Dignitatem and Veritatis
Splendor*.
Pope John XXII, 25
Pope Leo XIII, 100, 176
Pope Paul VI, 42–43, 49, 57,
147–51, 160, 208–9, 213. *See
also Humanae Vitae* and
Credo of the People of God.
Pope Pius IX, 77
Pope Pius XI, 144
Pope Pius XII, 49, 57, 179–80.
See also Humani Generis.
Pope Saint Pius X, 69, 73
Pope Vigilius I, 43
Pope, infallibility not
impeccability, 83–84
Pornography, 160–61
Positivism, legal, 165–69
Potter, Ralph B., 155
Pro, Blessed Miguel, 12–13,
169–70
"Pro-choice," 127–28

Prostitution, 169
Protestants, 86–88
Protoevangelium, 65–66, 72
Provan, Charles, 154
Proverbs, 113, 121
Prudence, virtue of, 113–14
Punishment, purposes of, 193–94
Purgatory, 24–25, 121

Quaker community, 76

Rape victims, treatment in
Catholic health care facilities,
181–82
Ratzinger, Cardinal Joseph,
Christianity, moralism and
communion, 129–30;
collaboration of men and
women, 136–37; conscience
and guilt, 103–4; definitive
teachings, 85, 88; God as
basis of human dignity, 54–55,
170; Iraq war, 201; loss of
God as root of hatred for
human life, 170–71; on the
origin of humanity, 47–49;
relativism, dictatorship of,
127–28; Tree of Life, man
crossing final boundary by
violating, 162, 164; war, 201
Reagan, Ronald, 95
Reality, material and spiritual,
20–25
Reason, and truth, 4, 14–19;
divine, 90; knowing about
God, 26–33; knowing about
ourselves, 9–13, 20–25;
relation to faith, 2, 9–13,
26–33, 206–7; speculative and
practical, 14–19, 92–93
Reasoning, 14–18
Rebellion, justified, 172, 175–76

Reconciliatio et Poenitentia, 122
Redemption, 65–72
Redemptoris Missio, 81
Reflection, 22–23
Reformation, the, 77–78, 143
Regina v. Dudley and Stephens, 183
Relation to others, 111–22
Relativism, 4–5, 127–28, 142–44
Religion, freedom of, 165
Reparation, 65–72
Response to Some Questions Regarding Certain Aspects of the Doctrine of the Church, 78
Revelation, 10–13, 25, 41–43, 90–91
Revolutionary War, American, 194
Rice, Charles E., 8, 18, 25, 32, 38–40, 100, 163, 171, 176, 183, 191–92, 204
Rice, Mary E., v, xi
Rich, Frank, 151, 164
Rights, origin and nature of, 165–70
Roberts, Andrew, 204
Roe v. Wade, 54–56, 166–67, 186–87
Romans, Letter to the, 26, 64, 72, 99, 110, 176
Rome, 56, 208
Rommen, Heinrich, 18, 100
Rosary, the, 99, 202–3, 211–12
Royal College of Physicians, 184

Sacramentum Caritatis, 213
Sacrosanctum Concilium, 80–81
Saint Alphonsus Ligouri, 71–72
Saint Augustine, 53–54, 58, 80, 105, 194
Saint Basil, 49
Saint Bonaventure, 100
Saint Gianna Beretta Molla, 125–27, 180
Saint Gregory of Nyssa, 130
Saint Gregory the Great, 73
Saint Irenaeus, 132
Saint John Chrysostom, 57
Saint John the Baptist, 203
Saint John Vianney, 26, 32
Saint John, Epistle of, 43
Saint John, Gospel of, 41–43, 66, 72–73, 80, 121, 176
Saint Joseph, 69
Saint Joseph's Seminary, 130–31
Saint Louis de Montfort, 211, 213
Saint Luke, Gospel of, 72–73, 77, 110, 122
Saint Margaret Clitherow, 118
Saint Mark, Gospel of, 73, 80, 122
Saint Mateo Correa Magallanes, 169–70
Saint Matthew, Gospel of, 41–43, 73, 80–81, 83, 88, 110, 122, 131, 213
Saint Maximilian Kolbe, 12–13, 118
Saint Maximus the Confessor, 73
Saint Monica, 53
Saint Paul, 26, 64, 68, 72–73, 80, 89, 99, 110, 121, 136–39. *See also Corinthians, First Letter to; Ephesians, Letter to the, Galatians, Letter to the, Hebrews, Letter to the, Philemon, Letter to,* and *Romans, Letter to the.*
Saint Peter, 76, 77, 84, 86, 107, 121
Saint Peter, Letters of, 121, 176
Saint Peter's Square, 203
Saint Thomas Aquinas, conversion of sinner, 194; free will, 128; God, existence of, 27–32, 35; heaven, 1; immortality of soul,

23–25; inclinations, human,
93–95; intellect, acts of,
17–18; killing or harming
another by private person,
175; knowing, 16–18;
knowing God through reason,
9, 27–29, 32; law, 89–90,
99–101, 159; law, natural,
89–101; law, unjust, 168–70;
love, 42–43; reason, specula-
tive and practical, 14–19,
92–93; relation in God, 111;
truth, 9–10; war, 198; wrong,
objective, 94–95
Saints, communion of, 120–21
Schiavo v. Schindler, 192
Schiavo, In re Guardianship of,
192
Schiavo, Michael, 188–91
Schiavo, Terri, 187–91
Schlidt, Andrea Matovina, 151
*Scott v. Sandford. See Dred Scott
Case.*
Scripture, Sacred, 10–11, 86–88,
90–91
Secularism, 143
Seewald, Peter, 162
Segregation, racial, 167–69
Self-defense, 172–76
Sex, culture and, 141–51, 161
Sheed, Frank J., 43, 73
Sheen, Fulton J., 5, 38, 40, 208,
213
Sin, actual, 63, 120; mortal and
venial, 63, 108–9, 120;
original, 52–53, 59–66; social,
118–20, 169; structures of,
118–20, 169
Sirach, 213
Skepticism, 14–16
Smith, William B., 183
Snead, O. Carter, 191

*Social Doctrine of the Church,
Compendium of the*, 122
Solidarity, 118–20
Soul, creation of, 47–48, 150–51;
immortality of, 23–25;
spiritual nature of, 20–25,
47–48, 150
Sound of Music, The, 3, 28
Spe Salvi, 117, 122
Speech, freedom of, 165
Spirit, divine, 18
Spirit, Holy, 11, 41–43, 78–80, 87,
89, 124–25
Spiritual distinguished from
material, 20–25
Stem cell research, embryonic,
161–62, 169
Stith, Richard J., 191
Sufficient reason, principle of,
26–29
Suicide, 155–56, 186
Sullivan, Joseph F., 38, 40
Sunday, 208
Supreme Court of the United
States, 55–56, 166–68, 186
Sydney, 212
Syllogism, 17

Talmadge, Eric, 204
Taylor, Frederick, 204
Taylor, Henry J., 30
Temperance, virtue of, 115
Teresa, Blessed, 57–58, 202, 208,
213
Terrorism, 194–95, 200–201
Tertio Millennio Adveniente, 213
Tiger, Lionel, 153
Timothy, First Letter to, 163
Tobit, Book of, 110, 213
Torode, Sam and Bethany, 151
Totalitarianism, 167
Tradition, 10–11, 86–88, 90–91

Trafficking in women and
    children, 169
Transplants, organ, 23–25
Transubstantiation, 208–10
Tree of Life, the, 162
Trese, Leo, 24–25, 43, 48–49, 64,
    73, 88
Trewhella, Matt, 154
Trinity, as model of family,
    119–25, 150–51. *See also*
    God, Trinity.
Truth, definition of, 9–10;
    freedom and, 128–31; God as,
    11; Jesus Christ as, 6; self-
    evident, 14–19; teaching of,
    5–7
U.S. v. Holmes, 183
Unitatis Redintegratio, 80–81
United Nations, 167
Utilitarianism, 190

Vatican Council, First (1869–
    1870), God, known through
    reason, 34–35, 39
Vatican Council, Second
    (1962–1965), apostolic
    succession, 77–78; baptism of
    desire, 89; Christ on dignity of
    human person, 56–57,
    111–12; Christ on person as
    relation, 111–12; Church,
    teaching authority of, 82–86,
    91, 195–96; gift of self, 2, 7,
    111–12, 123, 130; God,
    known through reason, 27, 32;
    God, known through universal
    belief, 31, 33; God, need for,
    8; man, dignity of, 58;
    Revelation, 11; Tradition, 11;
    war, 199–200. *See also Ad
    Gentes, Dei Verbum, Gaudium
    et Spes, Lumen Gentium,*

*Nostra Aetate, Sacrosanctum
    Concilium,* and *Unitatis
    Redintegratio.*
Vegetative state, persistent, 184,
    189–91
Veritatis Splendor, 97–98, 100,
    109–10, 131, 167
Violence, domestic, 141–42
Virtues, cardinal, 113–16;
    theological, 115–18

War crimes trials, 91–92, 189–90
War, American Revolutionary, 194
War, conscientious objection to,
    201–2; just, 172, 175–76,
    198–203; preventive, 201
Washington, George, 129, 194
Wertham, Frederic, 192
Wesley, John, 76, 154
Western culture, 2
Whitehead, Kenneth, 163
Will, freedom of the. *See* Free
    Will.
Willcocks, Raymond H., 204
Williams, Juan, 171
Williams, Roger, 76
Woman, as object, 160
Women, rights of, 136–39
Work, degrading conditions of,
    169
World Day of Peace, 200
World Trade Center, 199, 204
World War II, 4, 194, 204
World Youth Day, 54, 208, 211–12
Wrong, objective, 4–5, 93–101
Wuerl, Donald W., 64

Youth, and Pope Benedict XVI,
    112, 131, 206–13; and Pope
    John Paul II, x–xi, 54, 206–12